-KNiT-
A BOX OF
SOCKS

24 SOCK KNITTING PATTERNS FOR
YOUR DREAM BOX OF SOCKS

JULIE ANN LEBOUTHILLIER

DAVID & CHARLES

www.davidandcharles.com

CONTENTS

INTRODUCTION

To start, I would love to sincerely thank you for purchasing my book! My name is Julie Ann Lebouthillier, I'm a wife, mother to beautiful twin daughters and I'm the knitwear designer behind Twin Stitches Designs. As you may have guessed, our twin daughters were the inspiration behind the brand. I've designed over 150 patterns, with the majority of those being socks, and I love helping others knit and teaching them new skills. Some could say I have a passion for socks, and I'm certainly one of them.

For as long as I can remember sock knitting has been a passion of mine. The first project I ever decided to knit was an aran (worsted) weight pair of socks for my husband. Now, I have to admit my first pair wasn't as successful as I would have liked, but that's the magic of knitting. Everything can be fixed, you can rip out and try again. Over the years I've made hundreds of pairs of socks, and have been addicted to them ever since. Since that first 'bigfoot' pair of socks — if you can even call them that — I have perfected my sock knitting recipe.

There is something very magical about sock knitting, it not only provides warmth and comfort to your feet but also reflects your unique personality and creativity. There are endless possibilities with your yarn and needles. This book is more than just a compilation of some amazing knitting patterns, it's an invitation to explore the boundless creativity that knitting has to offer. Knitting is more than just a craft, it's a form of self-expression, a way to connect with others and the generations that came before us.

I had the honour to create this book as an inspiration for you to make your own box of socks, whether it will be for you, a loved one or a friend. You'll find this book has patterns for everyone. My hope is that this will spark your imagination and your passion to create all the socks you've always wanted. Grab your knitting needles and that skein of yarn that has been on your shelf for YEARS waiting to become a pair of socks. Yes we all know you have one of those (or 10) and then start turning the pages to start your own box of socks along with me.

Happy knitting & creating, friend!

Julie Ann Lebouthillier

TOOLS & MATERIALS

In this section you will find all the tools and materials necessary to knit your own pair of socks. I've also included some tips & tricks.

YARN

With so many incredible yarns on the market it's hard to decide which ones to pick for your socks. Here are a few things to keep in mind when you're looking to knit your next pair of socks.

CHOOSE THE RIGHT YARN

When you're working with sock yarns it's important to choose a yarn that is durable and hard-wearing. Look for yarn that has a high percentage of wool or other natural fibres, as these tend to hold up well over time. Choose the right yarn weight: when selecting yarn for your socks, choose a yarn that is appropriate for sock knitting. Look for yarns that are durable and have a high percentage of wool or other animal fibres. Sock yarns typically come in 4 ply (fingering) or 5 ply (sport weight), so choose a yarn that is appropriate for the pattern you plan to use.

TENSION (GAUGE) SWATCH

Always knit a tension swatch to ensure that you are using the correct needle size and yarn weight for the pattern. This will help you avoid any surprises in terms of sizing and fit. This can also help you see if the yarn you chose is a good match for the pattern. Some yarns may be too variegated to show off a delicate lace pattern.

MIX AND MATCH YARNS

If you don't have enough of one yarn to knit a whole pair of socks, consider mixing and matching different colours and textures to create a unique, one-of-a-kind pair of socks.

Use contrasting colours for heels and toes: If you are worried about not having enough yarn for the whole sock, consider using a contrasting colour for the heels and toes. This can create a fun and unique look while also stretching your yarn a bit further.

KEEP TRACK OF YARDAGE

Be sure to keep track of how much yarn you are using so you don't run out before you finish the second sock. Weigh your yarn before you start and after you finish each section of the sock (cuff, leg, heel, foot, toe) to keep track of how much yarn you are using.

GET CREATIVE

Don't be afraid to get creative and try out new stitch patterns or techniques. Sock knitting is a great way to experiment with different knitting techniques and create something truly unique.

SSK - SLIP SLIP KNIT

1. Slip the first stitch knitwise onto the right hand needle. (A)

2. Then slip the second stitch knitwise onto the right hand needle. (B)

3. Insert the tip of the left hand needle into the front loops and knit the two stitches together.

A

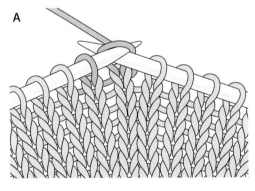

B

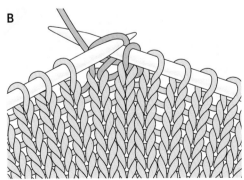

ABBREVIATIONS

Here you will find a list of abbreviations used all over the book.

1/1 LC: Slip 1 stitch onto cable needle, hold in front, k1, k1 from cable needle

2/2 LC: Slip 2 stitches onto cable needle, hold in front, k2, k2 from cable needle

3/3 RC: Slip 3 stitches onto cable needle, hold in back, k3, k3 from cable needle

3/3 LC: Slip 3 stitches onto cable needle, hold in front, k3, k3 from cable needle

2/2 RPC: Slip 2 stitches onto cable needle, hold in back, k2, p2 from cable needle

3/3 RPC: Slip 3 stitches onto cable needle, hold in back, k3, p3 from cable needle

CC: Contrast Colour

C: Colour

CO: Cast on

DPN: Double pointed needles

ds: Double stitch (Short rows), slip 1 stitch purlwise with yarn in front, bring yarn up, over and back to pull on the slipped stitch until it slides to show 2 legs, keep tension and work the next and following stitches as usual.

k: Knit

k tbl: Knit through the back loop

k2tog: Knit 2 stitches together (Decreased 1 stitch)

kfb: Knit front and back of the same stitch (Increase 1 stitch)

MC: Main Colour

p: Purl

p2tog: Purl 2 stitches together (Decreased 1 stitch)

RS: Right side

sl: Slip stitch

SSK: Slip, slip, knit the two stitches together (Decreased 1 stitch)

st(s): stitch(es)

WS: wrong side

yo: Yarn over

MEASURING AND ADAPTING PATTERNS

It was important for me to try and include as much information as I could in this book for you. As a knitting teacher the questions I get asked the most are; How many stitches should I cast on? What is negative ease and how much do I need? Don't worry I calculated it all for you! Opposite you'll find all the maths is done for you, you can find the exact number of stitches to cast on from baby all the way to adult large.

HOW TO MEASURE YOUR FOOT

FOOT LENGTH

Using a tape measure, place it on the floor. Position the back of the heel at the zero mark on the tape, then measure to the longest toe. You will want to subtract about 10% to allow for negative ease and a snug fit.

FOOT CIRCUMFERENCE

Using a tape measure to measure firmly around the circumference of the widest part of your foot. You will want to subtract about 10% to allow for negative ease and a snug fit.

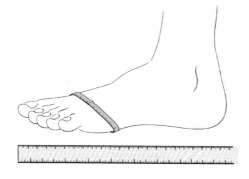

Pro Tip: *Most people like their foot and leg circumference the same.*

TIPS & TRICKS

Q: Do you have issues with your leg not fitting?

A: If the sock is too loose, go down a needle size to tighten your tension, as well as adding some ribbing on your leg. This will create a cozier fit to your leg overall.

If your sock is too tight, go up a needle size and also add some ribbing. The ribbing will help give your sock the stretch it needs to fit over your calf.

Q: How much negative ease should I have in my socks?

A: The rule of thumb is around 10% of negative ease for a pair of socks around the leg and largest part of your foot.

HOW MANY STITCHES TO CAST ON

Before you can cast on your pair of socks, you need to know your tension (gauge). The ideal tension of a pair of socks is firm and tight. This will ensure a longer wear on your socks, the looser the tension the more potential for holes.

To work out how many stitches you should cast on for your pair of socks, here's the calculation;

Total foot circumference - 10% for negative ease) x Tension stitches per 1in = CO stitches

Here's a cheat sheet with the tension stitches per inch by your overall foot circumference to know the approximate number of stitches you should cast on for your pair of socks. This only needs to be used for the socks without charts, which need to be the stated number of stitches for the chart repeats to work.

The total foot circumference includes the 10% of negative ease If you are in between sizes, please go down a size. Socks should always be tighter than looser.

TENSION STITCHES PER INCH

Foot Circ.	7	7½	8	8½	9	9½
7½in	52	56	60	64	68	72
8in	56	60	64	68	72	76
8½in	60	64	68	72	76	80
9in	64	68	72	76	80	84
9½in	66	72	76	80	84	88

CHILDREN'S FOOT SIZES

Are you looking to knit a pair of socks for a child instead of an adult? Use this table below to determine how many stitches to cast on for the size needed. You are able to use these numbers when knitting your pattern. Your heel stitches will be half of the amount of the cast-on stitches.

Shoe Size:	Fingering weight tension 9 sts per inch	DK weight tension 6 sts per inch	Approximate foot circumference
Baby 6-18 Months	36	24	4½
Toddler 2-3 Y	44	30	5½
Child 4-5 Y	48	32	6
Youth 6-9 Y	52	34	6½
Youth 10-13 Y	56	36	7

BASIC SOCK PATTERN

When I was writing this book it was important to me to include a basic sock pattern. You'll find tons of tips and tricks in this pattern on how to knit socks toe up and cuff down.

YARN OPTION

The sample was knitted using Tot le Matin Yarns TOT Stellina (75% Merino, 15% Nylon, 10% Stellina Bronze) light fingering weight, 100g (400m/437yds) in Figue.

NEEDLES

Size 2.25mm (US 1), or size needed to obtain tension, for your preferred method of knitting in the round.

OTHER TOOLS AND MATERIALS

- Stitch marker
- Darning needle
- Waste yarn for heel of toe up socks

TENSION (GAUGE)

unblocked

36 stitches and 40 rows measure 4 x 4in (10 x 10cm) over stocking (stockinette) stitch using 2.25mm needles

SIZES

Toddler (Child) (Adult Small) (Medium) (Large)

To fit a foot circumference of approximately: 4-5 (5-6) (6½) (7) (8)in / 10-13 (13-15) (16.5) (18) (20.5)cm

NOTES ON THE PATTERN

This pattern is written for a plain stocking stitch sock. You can add any type of texture to the pattern. You can also use any of these methods to turn a cuff down sock into a toe up.

TIPS ON HOW TO SWITCH A PATTERN TO TOE UP

First you'll need to determine the size you'd like to knit. For this example we will use a 56-stitch sock.

Use your preferred cast on for toe up socks (I used the Turkish cast on in this pattern) and increase to the toe number. This would be the number of stitches required for your pattern (Eg: 56 stitches)

If the foot is completed in stocking stitch, knit all stitches until you're ready to place the heel. If the sock has patterning you should start this pattern after the toe increases are completed.

Heel: You will be knitting until the foot measures 2in (5cm) less than your total foot length measurements going from the back of the heel to the end of the toes. You will measure from the cast-on stitches to the needles.

The two best heels for toe up socks are the Afterthought Heel and German Short Row. Both of these heels are included in the cuff down patterns. You will knit them as directed in the patterns.

Leg: You will continue to knit in pattern or stocking stitch until desired leg length before the ribbing.

Ribbing: Choose what type of ribbing you'd like for the pattern, (this could be: k1, p1 / k2, p2 or many more) Complete the ribbing for the number of rounds directed in the pattern and bind off using Jeny's Surprisingly Stretchy Cast (Bind) Off (see Techniques).

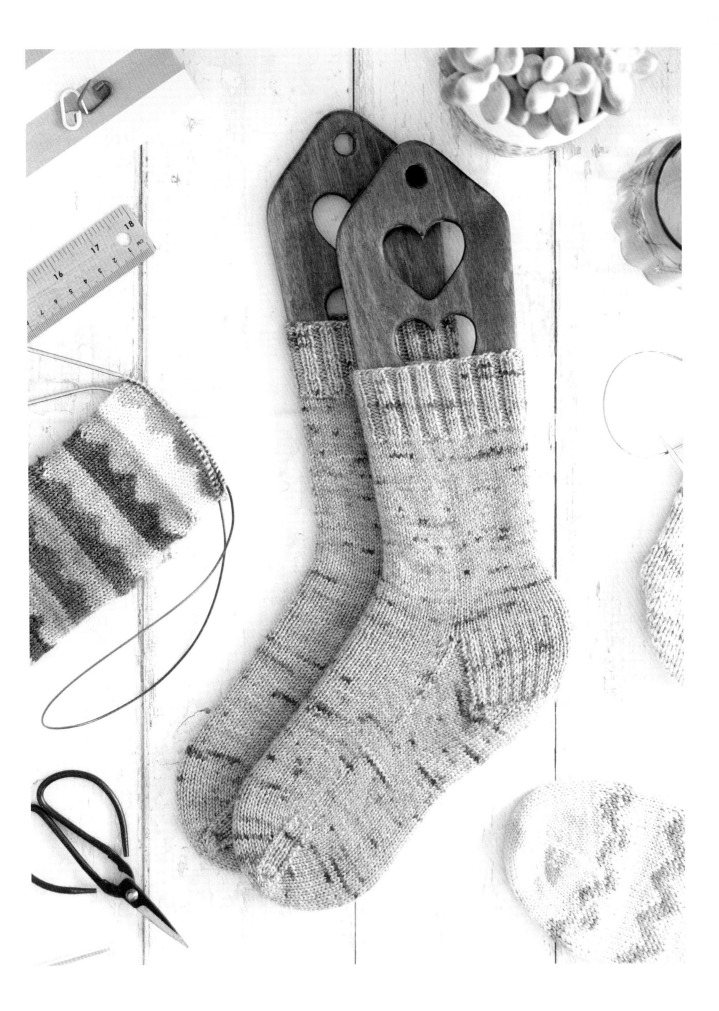

CUFF DOWN INSTRUCTIONS

CUFF

Using the long tail cast on (or preferred method) CO 40 (48) (56) (64) (72) sts. Join for working in the round taking care not to twist your sts, PM to mark the beginning of the round.

Magic Loop: Divide the sts evenly between your two needles 20 (24) (28) (32) (36) sts on each needle.

DPNS: Divide the sts evenly between your four needles 10 (12) (14) (16) (18) sts on each needle.

TODDLER AND CHILD SIZES

Rounds 1-10: *K2, p2; repeat from *.

ADULT SIZES

Rounds 1-14: *K2, p2; repeat from *.

LEG

Work in stocking stitch, knitting every round until you've reached the desired length from your cast-on edge. The sample was knitted to 6in (15cm) from the ribbing.

NOTE: My preferred length of leg is between 5½ to 7in (14 to 17.5cm) before starting the heel. You can make your sock leg as long or as short as you'd like.

HEEL

Heel is worked flat on Needle 1 or half the sts, 20 (24) (28) (32) (36).

Row 1 (RS): *Sl1, k1; repeat from * turn.

Row 2 (WS): Sl1, purl to end, turn.

Work Rows 1-2 a total of 10 (12) (15) (16) (16) times for a total of 20 (24) (30) (32) (32) rows.

HEEL TURN

Row 1 (RS): Sl1, k11 (14) (16) (18) 20), ssk, k1, turn.

Row 2 (WS): Sl1, p3 (5) (7) (7) (7), p2tog, p1, turn.

Row 3: Sl1, knit to one st before gap, ssk, k1, turn.

Row 4: Sl1, purl to one st before gap, p2tog, p1, turn.

Repeat rows 3 and 4 until all sts have been worked.

Knit across remaining heel stitches, pick up and knit 10 (12) (15) (16) (16) sts along the edge of heel flap. Pick up an extra stitch on the ladder between the stitches on the row below to close any gaps. Knit across instep stitches. Pick up 11 (13) (16) (17) (17) sts on the other gusset side starting with the extra stitch on the ladder between the stitches on the row below to close any gaps.

GUSSET

When decreasing gusset stitches, only work decreases on Needle 1 or back of heel. This is the needle (section) used to pick up all the gusset stitches. During these rounds, make sure to knit all stitches on Needle 2 (top of foot) without decreasing across the top of foot.

Round 1:

Needle 1: K1, ssk, knit to 3 sts before the end of row, k2tog, k1.

Needle 2: Knit all stitches.

Round 2:

Needle 1 and 2: Knit all stitches.

Repeat these two rounds until work returns to the original stitch count of 40 (48) (56) (64) (72) sts.

Continue knitting in pattern until you've reached 1¼ (1¼) (1¼) (1½) (1¾)in / 3 (3) (3) (4) (4.5)cm shorter than your foot length.

TOE

Round 1: K1, ssk, knit to the last 3 sts, k2tog, k1 (Repeat on both needles).

Round 2: Knit.

Magic Loop: Continue these two rounds until there are 10 (10) (12) (12) (12) sts left on each needle.

DPNS: Continue these two rounds until there are 5 (5) (6) (6) (6) sts left on each needle.

Graft together using the Kitchener stitch and weave in all ends. Block as desired.

Example: *My foot length is 9in (23cm). I usually knit a size small for my foot.*

I will take 9in (23cm) (total foot length) − 1¼in (3.5cm) (size small) = 7¾in (19.5cm)

I will knit 7¾in (19.5cm) from the heel before I start my toe.

PRO TIP: *How to measure your foot length for cuff down socks. Place a tape measure on the floor. Position the back of the heel at the zero mark on the tape, then measure to the longest toe. You will take this amount and subtract the amount of in/cm in the directions opposite.*

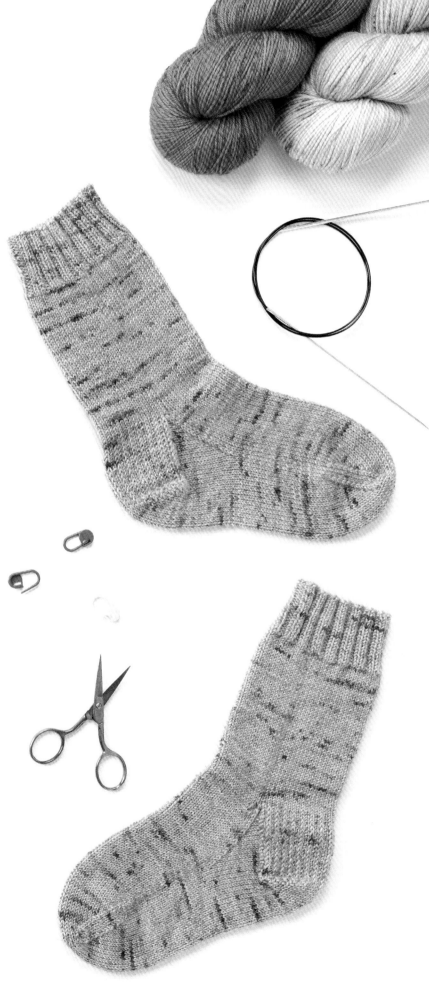

TOE UP INSTRUCTIONS

TOE

Using the Turkish cast on (or preferred method) and your MC, CO 16 (18) (20) (24) (28) sts: 8 (9) (10) (12) (14) sts each on the top and bottom needles.

Round 1: Knit all stitches.

Round 2: *K1, kfb, knit to the last two sts on needle, kfb, K1; repeat from * on the second needle.

Repeat these two rounds until you've reached 40 (48) (56) (64) (72) total sts: 20 (24) (28) (32) (36) sts each on the top and bottom needles.

Magic Loop: Divide the stitches evenly between your two needles 20 (24) (28) (32) (36) sts on each needle.

DPNS: Divide the stitches evenly between your four needles 10 (12) (14) (16) (18) sts on each needle.

FOOT

Work in stocking stitch, knitting every round until you've reached the required foot length. Place removable stitch marker or use waste yarn to mark location for heel.

Using waste yarn:

K20 (24) (28) (32) (36) sts using waste yarn in a contrast colour to your MC. Transfer those 20 (24) (28) (32) (36) sts back onto the left needle. K20 (24) (28) (32) (36) sts in your MC.

Work in stocking stitch, knitting every round until you have reached your desired leg length, measured from the removable heel marker or waste yarn. You will cut in your heel after finishing the cuff.

LEG

The sample was knitted to 6in (15cm) from the waste yarn before placing the cuff.

CUFF

TODDLER AND CHILD SIZES:

Rounds 1-10: *K2, p2; repeat from * around.

ADULT SIZES

Rounds 1-14: *K2, p2; repeat from * around.

PRO TIP: *If you find the front of your foot is always tight make sure to place 3-5 plain knit rounds before starting the decreases of the heel. For me, I personally like 3 knit rounds and I do 5 knit rounds for my husband.*

HEEL

Now that you've finished your cuff, return to the place where you put your waste yarn. Pick-up 20 (24) (28) (32) (36) sts each on rows below and above the contrast waste yarn. You will have 40 (48) (56) (64) (72) sts total for the heel. Remove the contrast waste yarn by picking out each stitch.

Cut the right leg of a stitch in the middle of the row in between your two needles. You will carefully remove the stitches on that row except the last two stitches on each side. Do not cut this yarn, you will use it to weave in any holes/ends later. Join your working yarn, use the tail to visually mark where your beginning of round is.

Round 1: *K1, ssk, knit to the last 3 sts on first needle, k2tog, k1; repeat from * on the second needle.

Round 2: Knit all stitches.

Magic Loop: Continue these two rounds until there are 10 (10) (12) (12) (12) sts left on each needle.

DPNS: Continue these two rounds until there are 5 (5) (6) (6) (6) sts left on each needle.

Cut the yarn leaving a 11¾in (30cm) tail and use the Kitchener stitch to graft the heel closed.

Weave in all your ends and do a happy dance! You finished a sock!

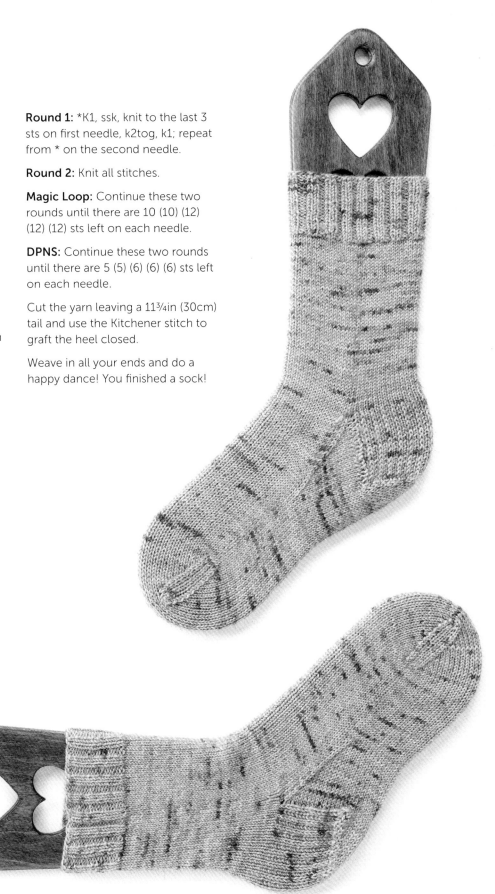

SOCK PROJECTS

APRIL SHOWERS

I wanted to play on the whimsical aspect of April Showers having clouds and a fade of blue rain falling down. This is such a fun and simple design; you can decide to use up any scraps and really make these socks your own! This design is knit cuff down using a heel flap and gusset.

YOU WILL NEED

NEEDLES
2.25mm (US 1) or size needed to obtain tension, for your preferred method of knitting in the round.

OTHER TOOLS AND MATERIALS
- Darning needle

YARN
The sample was knitted using MoonGlow Yarn Co Merino Nylon Sock yarn (75% Superwash Merino, 25% Nylon), fingering weight, 150g (635m/694yds) in April Showers Sock Set:

- MC: Silver Lining Gray (100g)
- CC: 5 x 10g mini skeins

SIZES
Adult Small (Adult Medium) (Adult Large)

To fit a foot circumference of approximately: 7 (8) (9)in / 18 (20.5) (23)cm

TENSION (GAUGE)
unblocked

32 stitches and 48 rows measure 4 x 4in (10 x 10cm) over stocking (stockinette) stitch using 2.25mm needles

CUFF

Using the long tail cast on (or preferred method) CO 56 (64) (72) sts. Join for working in the round taking care not to twist your stitches.

Magic Loop: Divide the stitches evenly between your two needles 28 (32) (36) sts on each needle.

DPNS: Divide the stitches evenly between your four needles 14 (16) (18) sts on each needle.

Rounds 1-12: *K2, p2; repeat from *.

PRO TIP: *If you're new to colourwork, try on the sock as you go to check the tension. If it's too tight you may need to go up a needle size. Carry the unused strands of yarn across the WS of the work, twisting yarn after every three or four stitches to avoid long loops of yarn on the WS.*

LEG

FOR ALL SIZES

Knit 2 rounds with your MC.

Start the colourwork chart on Row 1 and repeat the 14 (16) (18) st chart around the sock.

HEEL

Heel is worked flat over half the stitches. 28 (32) (36) sts.

Row 1 (RS): *Sl1, k1* repeat across.

Row 2 (WS): Sl1, purl across.

Work Rows 1-2 a total of 16 (16) (18) times for a total of 32 (32) (36) rows.

HEEL TURN

Row 1 (RS): Sl1, k16 (18) (20), ssk, k1, turn.

Row 2 (WS): Sl1, p7, p2tog, p1, turn.

Row 3 (RS): Sl1, knit to one st before gap, ssk, k1, turn.

Row 4 (WS): Sl1, purl to one st before gap, p2tog, p1, turn.

Repeat Rows 3 and 4 until all stitches have been worked.

Knit across remaining heel stitches. Pick up and knit 16 (16) (18) sts along the edge of heel flap. To close any gaps, pick up one extra stitch in the ladder between the corner of the heel flap and next needle. This will be referred to as Section 1.

Knit across the front of the foot. This will be referred to as Section 2.

Pick up an extra stitch in corner of Section 2 and heel flap, and then pick up and knit 16 (16, 18) sts along the second edge of heel flap. These stitches are added to Section 1. Finish knitting across Section 1.

GUSSET

When decreasing gusset stitches, only work decreases on Needle 1. This is the needle used to pick up all the gusset stitches. During these rounds make sure to knit all stitches on Needle 2 without decreasing across the top of foot.

Round 1:

Section 1: K1, ssk, knit to 3 sts before the end of needle, k2tog, k1

Section 2: Knit all stitches.

Round 2:

Section 1 and 2 : Knit all stitches.

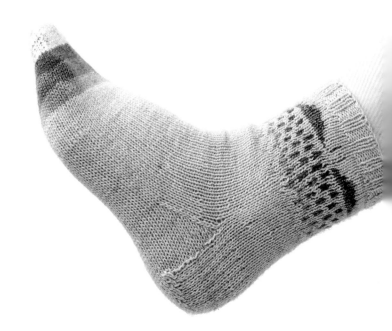

Continue Rounds 1 and 2 until you've reached the original stitch count of 56 (64) (72) sts.

FOOT

Continue knitting every stitch until the foot measures 3¼ (3½, 3¾)in / 8.25 (9, 9.5)cm shorter than the finished foot length.

To skip the colourwork before the toe, knit every stitch until it measures 1¼ (1½, 1¾)in / 3 (4, 4.5)cm.

Cut your MC and knit each stripe with a new CC, cutting the old CC.

Stripe 1: Knit 6 rounds with CC5.

Stripe 2: Knit 6 rounds with CC4.

Stripe 3: Knit 6 rounds with CC3.

Stripe 4: Knit 6 rounds with CC2.

Complete the toe in the MC.

TOE

Round 1: K1, ssk, knit to the last 3 sts, k2tog, k1 (work on both needles).

Round 2: Knit all stitches.

Continue rounds 1 and 2 until there are 12 (12) (12) sts on each needle. Graft together using the Kitchener stitch and weave in all ends.

CHARTS

Each square represents a stitch. Read all rows from right to left. Carry the unused strands of yarn across the WS of the work, twisting yarn after every three or four stitches to avoid long loops of yarn on the WS.

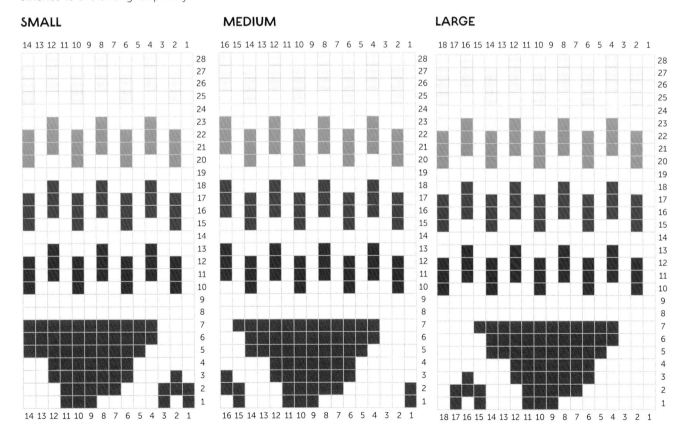

SMALL   MEDIUM   LARGE

KEY

MC   CC2   CC4
CC1   CC3   CC5

WAiTING FoR SNoWFALL

Every year I love designing a fun holiday sock pattern and Waiting for Snowfall is one of them. I love the simplicity of using a sock set and letting the colourwork and yarn shine together. You'll only need a 20g mini skein for the contrast details on this fun sock.

YOU WILL NEED

NEEDLES
Size 2.25mm (US 1), or size needed to obtain tension, for your preferred method of knitting in the round.

OTHER TOOLS AND MATERIALS
• Darning needle

YARN
The sample was knitted using Sweet Skein O'Mine Yarn (75% Merino, 25% Nylon), light fingering, 100g (423m/463yds) in Dashing Thru the Snow Sock Set.

• 100g and a 20g mini skein.

SIZES
Adult Small/Medium and Adult Large

To fit a foot circumference of approximately 8¼ (9)in / 21 (23)cm

TENSION (GAUGE)
unblocked

36 stitches and 40 rows measure 4 x 4in (10 x 10cm) over stocking (stockinette) stitch using 2.25mm needles

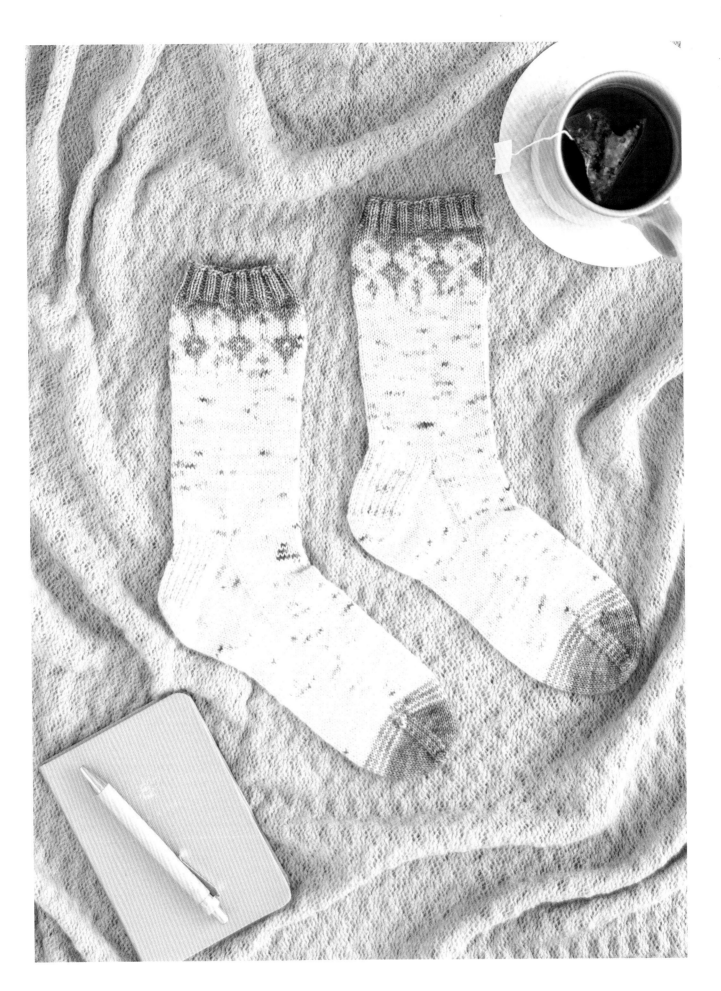

PATTERN

CUFF

Using the long tail cast on (or preferred cast on) with the CC, CO 60 (72) sts. Join for working in the round taking care not to twist your stitches.

Magic Loop: Divide the stitches evenly between your two needles 30 (36) sts on each needle.

DPNS: Divide the stitches evenly between your four needles 15 (18) sts on each needle.

Rounds 1-10: *K2, p2; repeat from *.

LEG

FOR SIZE LARGE ONLY

Set up Rounds:

Round 1: Knit all stitches.

Round 2: *K8, kfb; repeat from *. around until end of round bringing your stitch count to 80 sts.

FOR ALL SIZES

Start the colourwork chart and repeat around the sock. Please note: only work the 19 rounds of the chart once. Once completed, cut the CC and knit the rest with the MC.

FOR SIZE LARGE ONLY

Decrease Round:

Round 1: *K8, K2tog; repeat from *. around until end of round bringing your stitch count to 72 sts.

FOR ALL SIZES

Continue the sock in stocking (stockinette) stitch until desired length; Sample was knit to 6in (15cm) from the ribbing.

HEEL

The heel is worked on 30 (36) sts.

Row 1 (RS): *Sl1, k1; repeat from * across, turn.

Row 2 (WS): Sl1, purl to end, turn.

Repeat these two rows a total of 15 times (30 rows).

HEEL TURN

Row 1 (RS): Sl1, k17 (20), ssk, k1, turn.

Row 2 (WS): Sl1, p5, p2tog, p1, turn.

Row 3: Sl1, knit to one st before gap, ssk, k1, turn.

Row 4: Sl1, purl to one st before gap, p2tog, p1, turn.

Repeat rows 3 and 4 until all stitches have been worked.

Knit across and pick up 15 gusset sts. Pick up an extra stitch on the ladder between the stitches on the row below to close any gaps bringing the total number of stitches picked up to 16. Knit across instep stitches. Pick up 16 sts on the other gusset side starting with the extra stitch on the ladder between the stitches on the row below to close any gaps.

GUSSET

When decreasing gusset stitches, only work decreases on Section 1 or back of heel. This is the Section used to pick up all the gusset stitches. During these rounds make sure to knit all stitches on Section 2 (top of foot) without decreasing across the top of foot.

Round 1:

Section 1: K1, ssk, knit to 3 sts before the end of row k2tog, k1.

Section 2: Knit all stitches.

Round 2:

Section 1 and 2: Knit all stitches.

Repeat these two rounds until returning to the original stitch count 60 (72).

FOOT

Continue in stocking (stockinette) stitch until the work measures 1½in (1¾in) / 4 (4.5)cm shorter than the total foot length or desired negative ease.

FADING THE TOE

Round 1: Knit all the stitches in CC.

Round 2: Knit all the stitches in MC.

Complete Rounds 1-2 a total of three times. Proceed to the toe in your CC.

TOE

Round 1: K1, ssk, knit to the last 3 sts of section, k2tog, k1, repeat on second section.

Round 2: Knit.

Magic Loop: Continue these two rounds until there are 12 (12) sts left on each needle.

DPNS: Continue these two rounds until there are 6 (6) sts left on each needle.

Graft together using the Kitchener stitch and weave in all ends. Block as desired.

CHARTS

Each square represents a stitch. Read all rows from right to left. Carry the unused strands of yarn across the WS of the work, twisting yarn after every three or four stitches to avoid long loops of yarn on the WS.

SMALL/MEDIUM

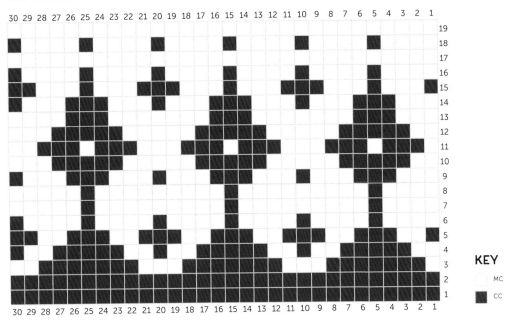

KEY

☐ MC
■ CC

LARGE

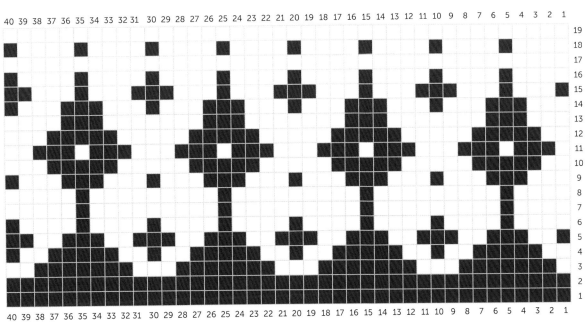

ALL YOU KNiT iS LOVe

Share your love of knitting with your nearest and dearest by knitting them the cutest socks. The name was inspired by the song 'All You Need Is Love' by the Beatles. This may be one of my favourite bands. Tell me you didn't start humming the tune as you read the name. I know I do. Using a DK-weight yarn, you'll knit these socks in no time! All You Knit is Love is knit cuff down, with a heel flap and gusset.

YOU WILL NEED

NEEDLES
Size 3.25mm (US 3), or size needed to obtain tension, for your preferred method of knitting in the round.

OTHER TOOLS AND MATERIALS
• Darning needle

YARN
The sample was knitted using The Discrete Unicorn DK Proper Sock (80% Superwash Merino, 20% Nylon), light worsted weight, 100g (225m/246yds) in Unicorn Dreams Sock Set.

• 100g and 20g mini skein.

SIZES
Adult Small (Adult Medium) (Adult Large)

To fit a foot circumference of approximately 7 (8) (8 ½)in / 18 (20.5) (21.5)cm

TENSION (GAUGE)
unblocked

24 stitches and 36 rows measure 4 x 4in (10 x 10cm) over stocking (stockinette) stitch using 3.25mm needles

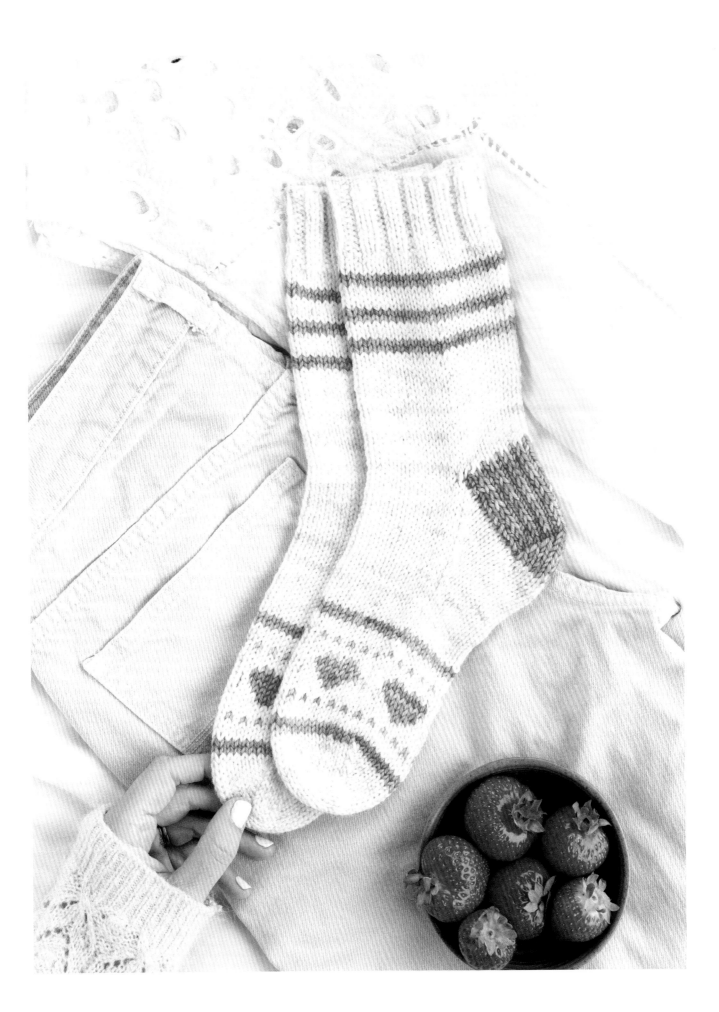

PATTERN

CUFF

Using the long tail cast on (or preferred method) CO 44 (48) (52) sts join for working in the round. Be careful not to twist your stitches.

Magic Loop: Divide the stitches evenly between your two needles 22 sts on each needle.

DPNS: Divide the stitches evenly between your four needles 11 sts on each needle.

Rounds 1-12: *K2, p2; repeat from *.

LEG

Rounds 1-3: Knit every stitch with your MC.

Rounds 4-5: Knit every stitch with your CC.

Rounds 6-9: Knit every stitch with your MC.

Rounds 10 and 11: Knit every stitch with your CC.

Repeat Rounds 6-11 once more.

Continue knitting in stocking (stockinette) stitch until you've reached the desired length from your cast-on edge. The sample was knitted to 6in (15cm) from the ribbing for the size Adult Small.

HEEL

Heel is worked flat with your CC on Needle 1 or half the stitches: 22 (24) (26).

Row 1 (RS): *Sl1, k1; repeat from *. to end, turn.

Row 2 (WS): Sl1, purl to end, turn.

Work Rows 1-2 a total of 12 (12) (13) times for a total of 22 (24) (26) rows.

HEEL TURN

Row 1 (RS): Sl1, k12 (14) (16), ssk, k1, turn.

Row 2 (WS): Sl1, p5 (7) (9), p2tog, p1, turn.

Row 3: Sl1, knit to one st before gap, ssk, k1, turn.

Row 4: Sl1, purl to one st before gap, p2tog, p1, turn.

Repeat rows 3 and 4 until all stitches have been worked. Cut your CC.

Knit across remaining heel stitches, pick up and knit 12 (12) (13) sts along the edge of heel flap. Pick up an extra stitch on the ladder between the stitches on the row below to close any gaps. Knit across instep stitches. Pick up 13 (13) (14) sts on the other gusset side starting with the extra stitch on the ladder between the stitches on the row below to close any gaps.

GUSSET

When decreasing gusset stitches, only work decreases on Section 1 or back of heel. This is the Section used to pick up all the gusset stitches. During these rounds make sure to knit all stitches on Section 2 (top of foot) without decreasing across the top of foot.

Round 1:

Section 1: K1, ssk, knit to 3 sts before the end of needle, k2tog, k1.

Section 2: Knit all stitches.

Round 2:

Section 1 and 2 : Knit all stitches.

Continue Rounds 1 and 2 until you've reached your original stitch count of 44 (48, 52) sts.

Continue knitting every stitch until the foot measures 3in (7.5cm) shorter than the finished foot length.

Continue knitting every stitch until you reach 3.5 (3.5, 3.5) inches / 9 (9, 9) cm shorter than your foot length.

Complete rows 1-22 with your MC and CC using the charted instructions. Cut your CC when completed.

To skip the colourwork before the toe, knit every stitch until it measures 2 (2, 2¼)in / 5 (5, 5.5)cm.

TOE

Round 1: K1, ssk, knit to the last 3 sts, k2tog, k1. (Repeat on both needles).

Round 2: Knit.

Magic Loop: Continue these two rounds until there are 10 sts left on each needle.

DPNS: Continue these two rounds until there are 5 sts left on each needle.

Graft together using the Kitchener stitch and weave in all ends. Block as desired. Stitch and weave in all ends.

CHARTS

Each square represents a stitch. Read all rows from right to left. Carry the unused strands of yarn across the WS of the work, twisting yarn after every three or four stitches to avoid long loops of yarn on the WS.

SMALL

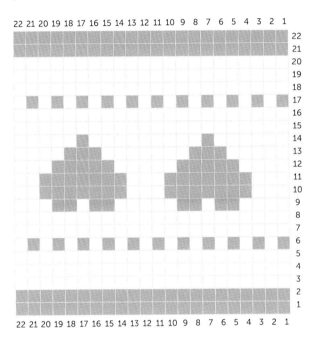

MEDIUM

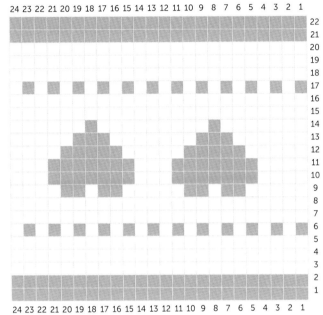

LARGE

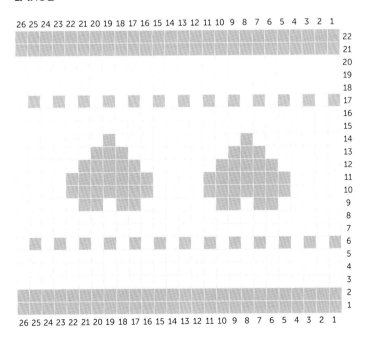

KEY

☐ MC

■ CC

DOWNSIDE UP

My go-to sock pattern for any DK-weight yarn, this is the perfect sock to knit up for all the family. It is designed to be worked cuff down, using just one skein of DK yarn, and features a heel flap and a gusset. Want to knit a toe up version? Check out the Upside Down pattern.

YOU WILL NEED

NEEDLES
Size 3.25mm (US 3), or size needed to obtain tension, for your preferred method of knitting in the round.

OTHER TOOLS AND MATERIALS
• Darning needle

YARN
The sample was knitted using Lolodidit USA DK (100% Superwash Merino Wool)light worsted weight, 115g (256m/280 yds) in Something Fall (1 skein).

SIZES
Toddler (Child) (Adult Small) (Adult Medium) (Adult Large)

To fit a foot circumference of approximately: 6 (6½) (7) (8) (8½)in / 15 (16.5) (18) (20.5) (21.5) cm

TENSION (GAUGE)
unblocked

24 stitches and 36 rows measure 4 x 4in (10 x 10cm) over stocking (stockinette) stitch using 3.25mm needles

PATTERN

CUFF

Using the long tail cast on (or preferred method) CO 36 (40) (44) (48) (52) sts. Join for working in the round taking care not to twist your stitches.

Magic Loop: Divide the stitches evenly between your two needles 18 (20) (22) (24) (26) sts on each needle.

DPNS: Divide the stitches evenly between your four needles 9 (10) (11) (12) (13) sts on each needle.

Rounds 1-10: *K2, p2; repeat from *.

LEG

Work in stocking stitch (knitting every round) until you've reached the desired length from your cast-on edge. The sample was knitted to 6in (15cm) from the ribbing.

HEEL

Heel is worked flat on Needle 1 or half the stitches 18 (20) (22) (24) (26).

Row 1 (RS): *Sl1, k1; repeat from *, turn.

ROW 2 (WS): Sl1, purl to end, turn.

Repeat these two rows a total of 8 (10) (12) (12) (13) times for a total of 16 (20) (22) (24) (26) rows.

HEEL TURN

Row 1 (RS): Sl1, k8 (10) (12) (14) (16), ssk, k1, turn.

Row 2 (WS): Sl1, p1 (3) (5) (7) (9), p2tog, p1, turn.

Row 3: Sl1, knit to one st before gap, ssk, k1, turn.

Row 4: Sl1, purl to one st before gap, p2tog, p1, turn.

Repeat rows 3 and 4 until all sts have been worked.

Knit across remaining heel stitches, pick up and knit 8 (10) (12) (12) (13) sts along the edge of heel flap. Pick up an extra stitch on the ladder between the stitches on the row below to close any gaps. Knit across instep stitches. Pick up 9 (11) (13) (13) (14) sts on the other gusset side starting with the extra stitch on the ladder between the sts on the row below to close any gaps.

GUSSET

When decreasing gusset stitches, only work decreases on Section 1 or back of heel. This is the Section used to pick up all the gusset stitches. During these rounds make sure to knit all stitches on Section 2 (top of foot) without decreasing across the top of foot.

Round 1:

Section 1: K1, ssk, knit to 3 sts before the end of row, k2tog, k1.

Section 2: Knit all stitches.

Round 2:

Section 1 and 2: Knit all stitches.

Continue Rounds 1 and 2 until work returns to the original stitch count of 36 (40) (44) (48) (52) sts.

Continue knitting in pattern until you've reached 1 (1½) (2) (2) (2¼)in / 2.5 (4) (5) (5) (5.5) cm shorter than your foot length.

TOE

Round 1: K1, ssk, knit to the last 3 sts, k2tog, k1 (Repeat on both needles).

Round 2: Knit.

Magic Loop: Continue these two rounds until there are 8 (8) (10) (10) (10) sts left on each needle.

DPNS: Continue these two rounds until there are 4 (4) (5) (5) (5) sts left on each needle.

Graft together using the Kitchener stitch and weave in all ends. Block as desired.

Plain socks are a great way to showcase your most colourful yarn!

UPSIDE DOWN

Are you looking for the perfect toe up sock recipe? Look no further, this pattern includes all sizes from Toddler to Adult Large. You'll be able to knit socks for the whole family. This design is knit toe up using an afterthought heel. Want to knit the cuff down version? Check out the Downside Up pattern.

YOU WILL NEED

NEEDLES
Size 3.25mm (US 3), or size needed to obtain tension, for your preferred method of knitting in the round.

OTHER TOOLS AND MATERIALS
• Darning needle

• Waste yarn (optional for heel)

YARN
The sample was knitted using Nicole C. Méndez on Soft Sock (80% Virgin Wool and 20% Nylon), light worsted weight, 100g (260m/284yds) in Expecto Patronum (1 skein).

SIZES
Toddler (Child) (Adult Small) (Adult Medium) (Adult Large)

To fit a foot circumference of approximately: 6 (6½) (7) (8) (8½)in / 15 (16.5) (18) (20.5) (21.5) cm

TENSION (GAUGE)
unblocked

24 stitches and 36 rows measure 4 x 4in (10 x 10cm) over stocking (stockinette) stitch using 3.25mm needles

PATTERN

TOE

Using the Turkish cast on (or preferred method) CO 16 (16) (20) (20) (20) sts: 8 (8) (10) (10) (10) sts each on the top and bottom.

Round 1: Knit all stitches.

Round 2: *K1, kfb, knit to the last two sts on needle, kfb, k1; repeat from * on the second needle.

Repeat these two rounds until you've reached 36 (40) (44) (48) (52) sts total: 18 (20) (22) (24) (26) sts each on the top and bottom needles.

Magic Loop: Divide the stitches evenly between your two needles 18 (20) (22) (24) (26) sts on each needle.

DPNS: Divide the stitches evenly between your four needles 9 (10) (11) (12) (13) sts on each needle.

LEG

Work in stocking stitch (knitting every round) until you reach required foot length. Place removable stitch marker or use waste yarn to mark location for heel.

Using waste yarn:

K18 (20) (22) (24) (26) sts using waste yarn in a contrast colour to your MC. Transfer those 18 (20) (22) (24) (26) sts back onto the left needle. 18 (20) (22) (24) (26) sts in your MC.

For the sample I knit 6½in (16.5cm) from the last round of increases of the toe. I placed my stitch marker to mark my heel and knit another 5in (13cm) for the leg before starting the ribbing.

You will continue knitting every round until you have reached your desired leg length, measured from the removable heel marker or waste yarn. You will cut in your heel after finishing the cuff.

CUFF

Rounds 1-14: *K2, p2; repeat from *.

Bind off using Jeny's Surprisingly Stretchy Cast (Bind) Off (see Techniques) or a stretch bind off of your choice.

HEEL

Now that you've finished your cuff, return to the place where you put your waste yarn. Pick up 18 (20) (22) (24) (26) sts each on rows below and above the contrast waste yarn. You will have 36 (40) (44) (48) (52) sts total for the heel. Remove the contrast waste yarn by picking out each stitch.

PRO TIP: *How to measure your foot length for toe up socks.*

Place a tape measure on the floor. Position the back of the heel at the zero mark on the tape, then measure to the longest toe. You will take this amount and subtract the amount of in / cm in the directions.

Total foot length − 1¾in (4.5cm) (Heel) − 1¾in (4.5cm) (Toe) = Amount needed to be knit for the foot before placing stitch marker.

Example: *my husband's total foot length is 10in (25.5cm). 10in − 1¾in (Heel)− 1¾in (Toe) = 6½in / 25.5cm − 4.5cm (Heel) − 4.5cm (Toe) = 16.5cm is where I will place his heel.*

Cut the right leg of a stitch in the middle of the row in between your two needles. You will carefully remove the stitches on that row except the last two stitches on each side. Do not cut this yarn, you will use it to weave in any holes/ends later. Join your working yarn, use the tail to visually mark where your beginning of round is.

Round 1: *K1, ssk, knit to the last 3 sts on first needle, k2tog, k1; repeat from * on the second needle.

Round 2: Knit all stitches.

Magic Loop: Continue these two rounds until there are 8 (8) (12) (12) (12) sts left on each needle.

DPNS: Continue these two rounds until there are 4 (4) (6) (6) (6) sts left on each needle.

Cut the yarn leaving a 11¾in (30cm) tail and use the Kitchener stitch to graft the heel closed.

PRO TIP: *Are you knitting these socks for little ones? You can try omitting the heels to make them into tube socks. This is great for growing little feet since they get longer before they get wider.*

I love textures and colourwork but sometimes knitting a great basic vanilla sock is an amazing palette cleanser.

FEELING SHEEPISH

Get ready to have everyone swooning over your socks! These are the socks you will want to show off to everyone. Feeling sheepish is knit cuff down with some stranded colourwork, featuring a German short row heel.

YOU WILL NEED

NEEDLES
Different sizes are made using the same number of stitches but different size needles.

- Small/Medium:

Size 2.25mm (US 1), or size needed to obtain gauge, for your preferred method of knitting in the round.

- Medium/Large:

Size 2.75mm (US 2), or size needed to obtain gauge, for your preferred method of knitting in the round.

YARN
The sample was knitted using Knit Picks Stroll (75% Fine Superwash Merino Wool, 25% Nylon) fingering weight, 50g (211m/231yds) in the following shades:

- MC: Dove Heather (25023) (2 balls)

- C1: White (26082) (1 ball)

- C2: Black (23701) (1 ball)

- C3: Everglade Heather (25607) (1 ball)

- C4: Burnt Umber Heather (29772) (1 ball)

SIZES
Small/Medium (Medium/Large)

To fit a foot circumference of approximately 7 (9) in / 18 (23)cm

TENSION (GAUGE)
unblocked

Size Small/Medium: 34 stitches and 36 rows measure 4 x 4in (10 x 10cm) over stocking (stockinette) stitch using 2.25mm needles

Size Medium/Large: 32 stitches and 34 rows measure 4 x 4in (10 x 10cm) over stocking (stockinette) stitch using 2.75mm needles

PATTERN

CUFF

Using the long tail cast on (or preferred method) CO 72 sts with your MC. Join for working in the round taking care not to twist your stitches,.

Magic Loop: Divide the stitches evenly between your two needles 36 sts on each needle.

DPNS: Divide the stitches evenly between your four needles 18 sts on each needle.

Rounds 1-20: *K2, p2; repeat from *.

LEG

Using the chart instructions you'll be completing Chart A on the front and back of your leg.

Once completed, cut your CCs and continue knitting the leg with your MC until you've reached approximately 6½in (16.5cm) from your cast-on edge or desired length.

HEEL

The short row heel is worked on half of your stitches.

Knit across the first 36 sts separating the stitches into three equal parts using stitch markers. Turn work.

Row 1 (WS): Ds, purl to the end, turn work.

Row 2: Ds, knit to the last ds but do not work it, turn work.

Row 3: Ds, purl to the last ds but do not work it, turn work.

Repeat Row 2 and 3 until you have worked all the stitches on each side of the stitch markers.

You have now completed the first half of the short row heel. In this section as you come to a ds you will knit or purl it together treating it as a single stitch. (Note; Depending on your stitch count if you finish on a knit round start on Row 2 instead of Row 1)

Row 1 (RS): Knit to the first ds, knit the ds together as one st, turn work.

Row 2: Ds, purl to the first ds, purl the ds together as one st, turn work.

Row 3: Ds, knit to the first ds, knit it together as one st, repeat with the next ds, turn work.

Row 4: Ds, purl to the first ds, purl it together as one st, repeat with the next ds, turn work.

Repeat Rows 3 and 4 until you have worked all the sts.

You are now ready to work in the round again. As your last row will be a WS row, knit one more round knitting all the ds stitches together as you come to them.

I recommend on the following two rounds to pick up an extra stitch or two in between the heel gaps. This will help close any holes that were created. Pick up the stitches between the gap and knit them together with the first stitch on your needle.

FOOT

Continue in stocking (stockinette) until the work measures 1½ (1¾)in / 4 (4.5)cm shorter than the total foot length or desired negative ease.

Using the chart instructions you'll be completing Chart B on all sts.

Once completed, cut your CCs and proceed to the toe with your MC.

TOE

Round 1: K1, ssk, knit to the last 3 sts, k2tog, k1 (Repeat on both needles).

Round 2: Knit all stitches.

Magic Loop: Continue these two rounds until there are 12 (12) sts left on each needle.

DPNS: Continue these two rounds until there are 6 (6) sts left on each needle.

> **PRO TIP:** *If you'd like to knit these toe up, use the Turkish cast on and refer to Measuring and Adapting Patterns on how to measure for your foot/leg. You'll read the chart in reverse starting from the top going down.*

CHARTS

Each square represents a stitch. Read all rows from right to left. Carry the unused strands of yarn across the WS of the work, twisting yarn after every three or four stitches to avoid long loops of yarn on the WS.

CHART A

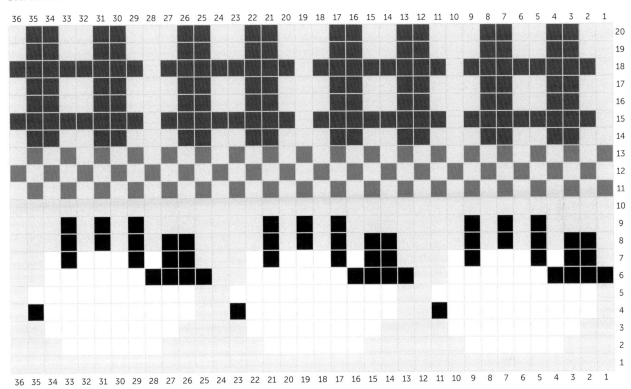

KEY

 MC

 C1

 C2

C3

C4

CHART B

PINEAPPLE CRUSH

Introducing the first fruit sock pattern is the pineapple pattern. With its simple diamond texture it's the next fun pattern in the collection. The socks are designed toe up and completed with a cute picot edging mimicking the top of a pineapple.

YOU WILL NEED

NEEDLES
Size 2.25mm (US 1), or size needed to obtain tension, for your preferred method of knitting in the round.

OTHER TOOLS AND MATERIALS
• Darning needle

• Waste yarn (optional for heel)

YARN
The sample was knitted using Campfiber Yarns Vibrant 80/20 (80% Superwash Merino, 20% Nylon) fingering weight, 100g (365m/400yds) 20g (71m/78yds) in the following shades:

• MC: Pineapple Delight (100g)

• CC1: Lucky (20g)

• CC2: Americano (20g)

SIZES
Adult Small (Adult Medium) (Adult Large)

To fit a foot circumference of approximately 7 (8) (8½)in / 18 (20.5) (21.5)cm

TENSION (GAUGE)
unblocked

36 stitches and 48 rows measure 4in x 4in (10 x 10cm) over stocking (stockinette) stitch using 2.25mm needles

PATTERN

TOE

Using the Turkish cast on (or preferred method) and CC1, CO 20 (24) (28) sts: 10 (12) (14) sts each on the top and bottom.

Round 1: Knit all stitches.

Round 2: *K1, kfb, knit to the last two sts on needle, kfb, k1; repeat from * on the second needle.

Repeat these two rounds until you've reached 56 (64) (72) total sts: 28 (32) (36) sts each on the top and bottom needles.

Magic Loop: Divide the stitches evenly between your two needles 28 (32) (36) sts on each needle.

DPNS: Divide the stitches evenly between your four needles 14 (16) (18) sts on each needle.

FOOT

Switching to your MC, using either the written or charted instructions, complete the chart on the top needle (half of your stitches) until you've reached the required foot length. Place removable stitch marker or use waste yarn to mark location for heel.

Using waste yarn:

K28 (32) (36) sts using waste yarn in a contrast colour to your MC. Transfer those 28 (32) (36) sts back onto the left needle. K28 (32, 36) sts in your MC.

You will continue knitting in pattern using either the written or charted instructions until you have reached your desired leg length, measured from the removable heel marker or waste yarn. You will cut in your heel after finishing the cuff.

LEG

The sample was knitted to 6in (15cm) before placing the cuff.

CUFF

The cuff is completed in your CC2.

Rounds 1-15: *K1, p1; repeat from *.

CREATING EDGING:

Step 1: K1, *insert the right needle in between the next 2 sts, wrap your yarn around right hand needle and pull through creating a stitch, place the stitch back on the left hand needle. Repeat from * 2 more times, creating 3 extra sts total.

Step 2: Knit and cast (bind) off 7 sts (first st, the 3 new sts and 3 sts)

Continue Step 1 and 2 until there are not enough stitches to work another repeat, cast off the remaining stitches as usual.

HEEL

Now that you've finished your cuff, return to the place where you put your waste yarn. Pick up 28 (32) (36) sts each on rows below and above the contrast waste yarn. You will have 56 (64) (72) sts total for the heel. Remove the contrast waste yarn by picking out each stitch.

Cut the right leg of a stitch in the middle of the row in between your two needles. You will carefully remove the stitches on that row except the last two stitches on each side. Do not cut this yarn, you will use it to weave in any holes/ends later. Join your working yarn, use the tail to visually mark where your beginning of round is.

Round 1: *K1, ssk, knit to the last 3 sts on first needle, k2tog k1; repeat from * on the second needle.

Round 2: Knit all stitches.

Magic Loop: Continue these two rounds until there are 10 (12) (14) sts left on each needle.

DPNS: Continue these two rounds until there are 5 (6) (7) sts left on each needle.

Cut the yarn leaving a 12in (30.5cm) tail and use the Kitchener stitch to graft the heel closed.

Weave in all your ends and do a happy dance! You finished a sock!

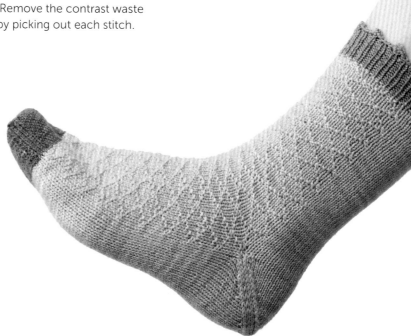

CHART

Each square represents a stitch. Read all rows from right to left.

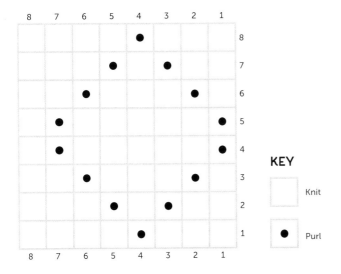

KEY

☐ Knit

● Purl

WRITTEN INSTRUCTIONS:

Round 1: K3, p1, k4.

Round 2: K2, p1, k1, p1, k3.

Round 3: K1, p1, k3, p1, k2.

Rounds 4-5: P1, k5, p1, k1.

Round 6: Repeat Round 3.

Round 7: Repeat Round 2.

Round 8: Repeat Round 1.

Repeat Rounds 1-8 on the front of the sock only.

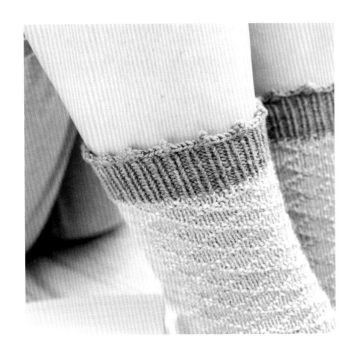

PRO TIP: *Do you have trouble with remembering chart repeats? Place a different colour stitch marker every 8 stitches in between the repeats. This will help you avoid any mistakes.*

JUICY WATERMELON

This pair of socks was designed back in the summer of 2022 and is still one of my favourite knits. The fun bright watermelon colours with the colourwork seeds is the perfect summer-time project. Grab your pair of socks and enjoy the summer sun!

YOU WILL NEED

NEEDLES

Size 2.25mm (US 1), or size needed to obtain tension, for your preferred method of knitting in the round.

OTHER TOOLS AND MATERIALS

• Darning needle

YARN

The sample was knitted using MoonGlow Yarn Co Merino Nylon Sock yarn (75% Superwash Merino, 25% Nylon), fingering weight, 130g (550m/601yds) in the Watermelon Sugar mini skein set:

• C1: Fresh off the vine (deep green) (20g)

• C2: Zest (medium green) (20g)

• C3: Frozen Margarita (light green) (20g)

• C4: Sugar Baby (light pink) (20g)

• C5: Watermelon Sugar (medium pink) (20g)

• C6: Juicy (deep red) (20g)

• C7: Black diamond (black) (10g)

SIZES

Toddler (Child) (Adult Small) (Adult Medium) (Adult Large)

To fit a foot circumference of approximately: 4-5 (5-6) (6½) (7) (8)in / 10-13 (13-15) (16.5) (18) (20.5)cm

TENSION (GAUGE)

unblocked

32 stitches and 42 rows measure 4 x 4in (10 x 10cm) over stocking (stockinette) stitch using 2.25mm needles

PATTERN

CALCULATING HOW LONG TO MAKE THE REPEATS

Place a tape measure on the floor. Position the back of the heel at the zero mark on the tape, then measure to the longest toe. This is the total foot length.

Take your total foot length plus your desired leg length and divide this by 12 (number of colour sections 6 on the foot and 6 on the leg) = The amount you'll be knitting each repeat. This can be calculated in cm or in to give an approximate length for each repeat.

CUFF

Using the long tail cast on (or preferred stretchy cast on) CO with C1 40 (48) (56) (64) (72) sts. Join for working in the round taking care not to twist your stitches.

Magic Loop: Divide the stitches evenly between your two needles 20 (24) (28) (32) (36) sts on each needle.

DPNS: Divide the stitches evenly between your four needles 10 (12) (14) (16) (18) sts on each needle.

Rounds 1-10: *K2, p2tbl; repeat from *.

LEG

Work in stocking stitch, knitting every round until you've reached the desired length for the yarn shade as calculated earlier. (The sample was knitted to approximately 1¼in (3cm) each colour).

Colour change round: Switching colours *K1, sl1; repeat from *.

Continue with in this manner until you've reached C4 (medium pink), then you will be completing the colourwork chart at the same time as the pattern instructions. This will create the seeds in the watermelon.

The seeds will only be in the sections with C5 and C6, creating the seeds in the middle of the watermelon.

HEEL

Knit across the first 20 (24) (28) (32) (36) sts separating the stitches into three parts using stitch markers. If your stitch count isn't divisible by 3, then the middle section gets more stitches. (Eg. If it's 28, then divide it as 9 / 10 / 9) Turn work.

Row 1 (WS): Ds, purl to the end, turn work.

Row 2 (RS): Ds, knit to the last ds but do not work it, turn work.

Row 3: Ds, purl to the last ds but do not work it, turn work.

Repeat Row 2 and 3 until you have worked all the stitches on each side of the stitch markers.

You have now completed the first half of the short row heel. In this section as you come to a ds you will knit or purl it together treating it as a single stitch. (Note; Depending on your stitch count if you finish on a knit round start on Row 2 instead of Row 1)

Row 1 (RS): Knit to the first ds, knit the ds together as one st, turn work.

Row 2 (WS): Ds, purl to the first ds, purl the ds together as one st, turn work.

Row 3: Ds, knit to the first ds, knit it together as one st, repeat with the next ds, turn work.

Row 4: Ds, purl to the first ds, purl it together as one st, repeat with the next ds, turn work.

Repeat Rows 3 and 4 until you have worked all the stitches.

You are now ready to work in the round again. As your last row will be a WS row, knit one more round knitting all the ds together as you come to them.

I recommend on the following two rounds to pick up an extra stitch or two in between the heel gaps. This will help close any holes that were created. Pick up the stitches between the gap and knit them together with the first stitch on your needle.

FOOT

Continue working in the pattern completing the colourwork in C5 and C6. For the foot you will be doing the colours in opposite order from the cast on. Going from the deep red to the green.

Work in stocking stitch, knitting every round until you've reached the desired length for the yarn shade as calculated earlier. (The sample was knitted to approximately 1¼in (3cm) each colour).

Colour change round: Switching colours *K1, sl1; repeat from *.

Continue with in this manner until you've reached C1 (deep green).

TOE

The toe will be completed in your C1 (deep green).

Round 1: K1, ssk, knit to the last 3 sts, k2tog, k1 (Repeat on both needles).

Round 2: Knit all stitches.

Magic Loop: Continue these two rounds until there are 8 (10) (12) (12) (14) sts left on each needle.

DPNS: Continue these two rounds until there are 4 (5) (6) (6) (7) sts left on each needle.

Cut the yarn leaving a 11¾in (30cm) tail and use the Kitchener stitch to graft the heel closed and weave in all ends. Block as desired.

CHART

Each square represents a stitch. Read all rows from right to left. Carry the unused strands of yarn across the WS of the work, twisting yarn after every three or four stitches to avoid long loops of yarn on the WS.

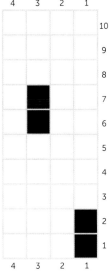

KEY

□ CC 5 & 6

■ CC7

When in doubt, knit socks — it's a step in the right direction.

DOUBLE THE FUN

Have you ever wanted to use up those beautiful skeins of fingering weight yarn but are too intimidated to try using it single stranded? This is the pattern for you! For this pattern you will knit the socks double stranded, which means you will be holding two strands of fingering weight in your hand instead of one. This creates a squishy and amazing fabric to knit with, it also goes WAY faster!

YOU WILL NEED

NEEDLES
Size 3.5mm (US 4), or size needed to obtain tension for your preferred method of knitting in the round.

OTHER TOOLS AND MATERIALS
• Darning needle

YARN
The sample was knitted using TOT le Matin Yarns (75% Superwash Merino, 25% Nylon) fingering weight, 100g (425m/464yds) in the following shades:

• MC: POP light (1 skein)

• CC: Aquamarine (only a small amount needed – I used a 20g mini skein)

SIZES
Toddler (Child) (Adult Small) (Adult Medium) (Adult Large) (Adult X-Large)

To fit a foot circumference of approximately: 5½ (6½) (7) (8) (8½) (9½)in / 14 (16.5) (18) (20.5) (21.5) (24)cm

TENSION (GAUGE)
unblocked

22 stitches and 32 rows measure 4 x 4in (10 x 10cm) over stocking (stockinette) stitch using 3.5mm needles

PATTERN

ABOUT THE PATTERN

Here are some tips to keep in mind when you're knitting with fingering weight held double for the first time

- Check your tension, all fingering weight yarns have different thickness and sizes. Some can be on the thinner side or thicker.

- Notes on tension: if you have too many stitches you need to go up a needle size. If you don't have enough stitches you need to go down a size needle.

- Don't want to knit double stranded? No worries you can use any worsted weight yarn instead.

- This would be an amazing project for using up any mini skeins! Pick a colour for your base and change up the mini skeins every 6-8 rounds to create an amazing marled unique pair of socks.

CUFF

Holding the CC yarn double, using the long tail cast on (or preferred method) CO 32 (36) (40) (44) (48) (52) sts. Join for working in the round taking care not to twist your stitches.

Magic Loop: Divide the stitches evenly between your two needles 16 (18) (20) (22) (24) 26) sts on each needle.

DPNS: Divide the stitches evenly between your four needles 8 (9) (10) (11) (12) (13) sts on each needle.

Rounds 1 and 2: *K2, p2; repeat from *.

Cut your CC and switch to MC.

Round 3: Knit all stitches.

Rounds 4-10: *K2, p2; repeat from *.

LEG

Continue knitting in stocking stitch until you've reached 3½ (4) (6) (6) (6) (6)in / 9 (10) (15) (15) (15) (15) cm, or the desired length from your cast-on edge. The sample was knitted to 6in (15cm) from the ribbing for the size Adult Small.

HEEL

The short row heel is worked on half of your sts.

Knit across the first 16 (18) (20) (22) (24) 26) sts separating the stitches into three equal parts using stitch markers. If your stitch count isn't divisible by 3, then the middle section gets more stitches. (Eg; If it's 20, then divide it as 6 / 8 / 6) Turn work.

Row 1 (WS): Ds, purl to the end, turn work.

Row 2 (RS): Ds, knit to the last ds but do not work it, turn work.

Row 3: Ds, purl to the last ds but do not work it, turn work.

Repeat Row 2 and 3 until you have worked all the stitches on each side of the stitch markers.

You have now completed the first half of the short row heel. In this section as you come to a ds you will knit or purl it together treating it as a single stitch. (Note; Depending on your stitch count if you finish on a knit round start on Row 2 instead of Row 1).

Row 1 (RS): Knit to the first ds, knit the ds together as one st, turn work.

Row 2 (WS): Ds, purl to the first ds, purl the ds together as one st, turn work.

Row 3: Ds, knit to the first ds, knit it together as one st, repeat with the next ds, turn work.

Row 4: Ds, purl to the first ds, purl it together as one st, repeat with the next ds, turn work.

Repeat Rows 3 and 4 until you have worked all the stitches.

You are now ready to work in the round again. As your last row will be a WS row, knit one more round knitting all the ds together as you come to them.

I recommend on the following two rounds to pick up an extra stitch or two in between the heel gaps. This will help close any holes that were created. Pick up the stitches between the gap and knit them together with the first stitch on your needle.

Continue knitting in pattern until you've reached 1 (1½) (2) (2) (2) (2¼)in / 2.5 (4) (5) (5) (5) (5.5)cm shorter than your foot length.

TOE

Round 1: K2, ssk, knit to the last 4 sts, k2tog, k2 (Repeat on both needles).

Round 2: Knit all stitches.

Magic Loop: Continue these two rounds until there are 8 (8) (10) (10) (10) (10) sts left on each needle.

DPNS: Continue these two rounds until there are 4 (4) (5) (5) (5) (5) sts left on each needle.

Graft together using the Kitchener stitch and weave in all ends. Block as desired.

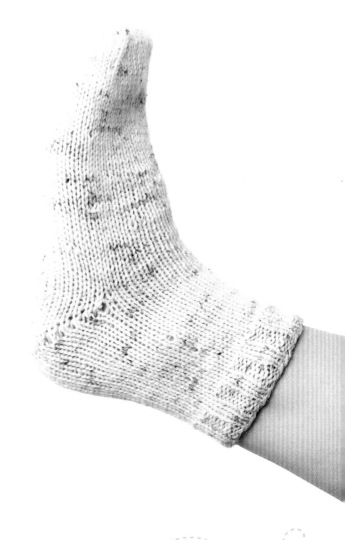

Socks are the perfect small portable knitting project to take everywhere with you.

BIRTHDAY SPRINKLES

Have you ever dreamed about a pair of socks? Yes, this does happen to some of us! I envisioned this fun pair of sprinkle socks, reminding me of my birthday cakes growing up with the white frosting that had the sprinkles already in it. This fun simple pair of socks is first completed only with the two colours then you'll add the sprinkles using simple embroidery.

YOU WILL NEED

NEEDLES
Size 2.25mm (US 1), or size needed to obtain tension, for your preferred method of knitting in the round.

OTHER TOOLS AND MATERIALS
• Stitch marker
• Darning needle

YARN
The sample was knitted using Campfiber Yarns (80% Superwash Merino, 20% Nylon), fingering weight, 100g (365m/400yds) in the following shades:

• MC: Barbie (1 skein)
• CC: Bare (20g mini skein)
• 6 different colours of scrap yarn for the sprinkles in fingering weight

SIZES
Adult Small (Adult Medium) (Adult Large)

To fit a foot circumference of approximately: 7 (8) (9)in / 18 (20.5) (23)cm

TENSION (GAUGE)
unblocked

36 stitches and 40 rows measure 4 x 4in (10 x 10cm) over stocking (stockinette) stitch using 2.25mm (US 1) needles

PATTERN

CUFF

Using the long tail cast on (or preferred cast on) with the CC, CO 56 (64) (72) sts. Join for working in the round taking care not to twist your stitches.

Magic Loop: Divide the stitches evenly between your two needles 28 (32) (36) sts on each needle.

DPNS: Divide the stitches evenly between your four needles 14 (16) (18) sts on each needle.

Rounds 1-14: *K2, p2; repeat from *.

Rounds 15-20: Knit all stitches.

Round 21: Decrease evenly 0 (1) (2) sts around. You will now have 56 (63, 70) sts.

LEG

FOR ALL SIZES

Start the Leg colourwork chart and repeat the 7 st pattern around the sock. Please note: only work the 5 rounds of the chart once. Once completed, cut the CC and knit the rest with the MC.

Increase Round: Increase evenly 0 (1) (2) sts around. You will now have 56 (64) (72) sts.

Continue the sock in stocking stitch until desired length; sample was knit to 6in (15cm) from the ribbing.

HEEL

The heel is worked on needle 1 or 28 (32) (36) sts.

Row 1 (RS): *Sl1, k1; repeat from *, turn.

Row 2 (WS): Sl1, purl across, turn.

Repeat these two rows a total of 15 times (30 rows).

HEEL TURN

Row 1 (RS): Sl1, k16 (18) (20), ssk, k1, turn.

Row 2 (WS): Sl1, p5, p2tog, p1, turn.

Row 3: Sl1, knit to one st before gap, ssk, k1, turn.

Row 4: Sl1, purl to one st before gap, p2tog, p1, turn.

Repeat Rows 3 and 4 until all stitches have been worked.

Knit across and pick up 15 gusset sts. Pick up an extra stitch on the ladder between the stitches on the row below to close any gaps bringing the total number of stitches picked up to 16. Knit across instep sts. Pick up 16 sts on the other gusset side starting with the extra stitch on the ladder between the stitches on the row below to close any gaps.

GUSSET

When decreasing gusset stitches, only work decreases on Section 1 or back of heel. This is the Section used to pick up all the gusset stitches. During these rounds make sure to knit all stitches on Section 2 (top of foot) without decreasing across the top of foot.

Round 1:

Section 1: K1, ssk, knit to 3 sts before the end of row k2tog, k.

Section 2: Knit all stitches.

Round 2:

Section 1 and 2: Knit all stitches.

Repeat these two rounds until returning to the original st count of 56 (64) (72).

Continue in stocking stitch until the work measures 1½ (1¾) (2)in / 4 (4.5) (5)cm shorter than the total foot length or desired negative ease.

TOE

Decrease Round: Decrease evenly 0 (1) (2) sts around. You will now have 56 (63) (70) sts.

FOR ALL SIZES

Start the foot colourwork chart and repeat the 7 st pattern around the sock. Please note: only work the 5 rounds of the chart once. Once completed, cut the MC and knit the rest with the CC.

Increase Round: Increase evenly 0 (1) (2) sts around. You will now have 56 (64) (72) sts.

Round 1: K1, ssk, knit to the last 3 sts of section, k2tog, k1. (Repeat on both sections).

Round 2: Knit.

Magic Loop: Continue these two rounds until there are 10 (12) (12) sts left on each needle.

DPNS: Continue these two rounds until there are 5 (6) (6) sts left on each needle.

Graft together using the Kitchener stitch and weave in all ends. Block as desired.

SPRINKLES

Once the socks are completed you will be adding the sprinkles. These are done using scraps of yarn of the same weight. They will be embroidered onto your sock.

You will be using a darning needle and some scrap yarn for the colour of the sprinkle.

Step 1: Start by fastening your yarn at the back of the work. Poke your needle through the right side of the fabric bringing the yarn through.

Step 2: Insert the needle under both 'legs' of the st diagonal to it and pull the yarn through.

Step 3: Insert the needle into the bottom of the stitch you've finishing and let it come out at the bottom of the next st.

Repeat Step 2 and 3 on the same sprinkle. Each sprinkle on the sample was embroidered twice in the same st.

Make sure to keep the yarn tension even.

Repeat these steps to create your sprinkles. Make as many as you'd like on your sock.

When working colourwork socks always remember to carry your floats over 3-4 stitches.

CHARTS

Each square represents a stitch. Read all rows from right to left. Carry the unused strands of yarn across the WS of the work, twisting yarn after every three or four stitches to avoid long loops of yarn on the WS.

LEG CHART

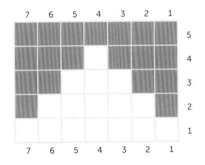

KEY

 MC

 CC

FOOT CHART

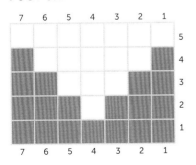

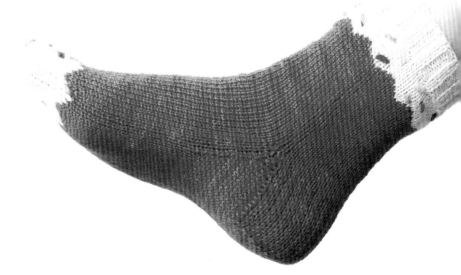

SPRING ROSES

I wanted to include a fun shorty pair of socks inspired by spring flowers. I love the simplicity of this lace texture mixed with the beautiful speckles of the yarn. It's the perfect pair of socks to cast on when you start to feel the warm weather of spring arriving.

YOU WILL NEED

NEEDLES
Size 4mm (US 6), or size needed to obtain tension, for your preferred method of knitting in the round.

OTHER TOOLS AND MATERIALS
• Darning needle

YARN
The sample was knitted using Tot le Matin Yarns in TOT Sock (75% Merino Wool, 25% Nylon), fingering weight, 100g (425m/464yds) in Fruite (1 skein).

SIZES
Adult Small (Adult Medium) (Adult Large)

To fit a foot circumference of approximately: 7 (8) (8½)in / 18 (20.5) (21.5)cm

TENSION (GAUGE)
unblocked

20 stitches and 28 rows measure 4 x 4in (10 x 10cm) over stocking (stockinette) stitch using 4mm (US 6) needles

PATTERN

TOE

Using the Turkish cast on (or preferred method) and holding your yarn double, CO 20 sts; 10 sts each on top and bottom needles.

Round 1: Knit all stitches.

Round 2: *K1, kfb, knit to the last two sts on needle, kfb, k1; repeat from * on the second needle.

Repeat these two rounds until you've reached 40, 44, 48 sts total.

Magic Loop: Divide the stitches evenly between your two needles 20 (22) (24) sts on each needle. The first needle will be Section 1 or the front of your foot while needle 2 will be Section 2 or the bottom of your foot.

DPNS: Divide the stitches evenly between your four needles 10 (11) (12) sts on each needle. The first two needles will be Section 1 or the front of your foot, the third and fourth needle will be Section 2 or the bottom of your foot.

FOOT

Use either the written or charted instructions for Section 1.

For Needle 2: Knit all stitches.

Repeat the written or charted instructions until you reach required foot length.

HEEL

The short row heel is worked on Section 2, which is half of your stitches.

Knit across the first 20 (22) 56(24) sts separating the stitches into three parts using stitch markers. If your stitch count isn't divisible by 3, then the middle section gets more stitches. (Eg; If it's 22, then divide it as 7 / 8 / 7) Turn work.

Row 1 (WS): Ds, purl to the end, turn work.

Row 2 (RS): Ds, knit to the last ds but do not work it, turn work.

Row 3: Ds, purl to the last ds but do not work it, turn work.

Repeat Rows 2 and 3 until you have worked all the stitches on each side of the stitch markers.

You have now completed the first half of the short row heel. In this section as you come to a ds you will knit or purl it together treating it as a single stitch. (Note; Depending on your stitch count if you finish on a knit round start on Row 2 instead of Row 1).

Row 1 (RS): Knit to the first ds, knit the ds together as one st, turn work.

Row 2 (WS): Ds, purl to the first ds, purl the ds together as one st, turn work.

Row 3: Ds, knit to the first ds, knit it together as one st, repeat with the next ds, turn work.

Row 4: Ds, purl to the first ds, purl it together as one st, repeat with the next ds, turn work.

Repeat Rows 3 and 4 until you have worked all the stitches.

You are now ready to work in the round again. As your last row will be a WS row, knit one more round knitting all the ds together as you come to them.

I recommend on the following two rounds to pick up an extra stitch or two in between the heel gaps. This will help close any holes that were created. Pick up the stitches between the gap and knit them together with the first stitch on your needle.

LEG

Use either the written or charted instructions for Section 1.

For Section 2: Knit all stitches.

Repeat the written or charted instructions until you reach the desired leg length. The sample was knitted 1½in (4cm) from the heel before knitting the cuff.

CUFF

Rounds 1-10: *K2, p2; repeat from *.

Bind Off using Jeny's Surprisingly Stretchy Cast (Bind) off (see Techniques).

CHARTS

Each square represents a stitch. Read all rows from right to left.

SMALL

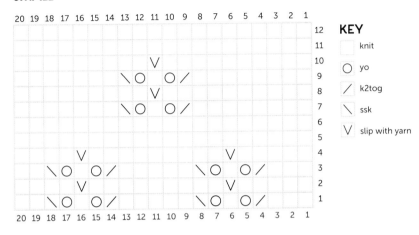

MEDIUM

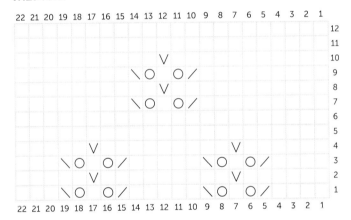

LARGE

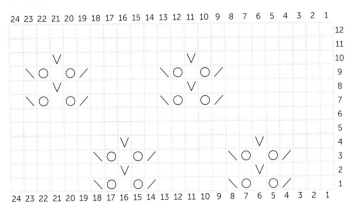

KEY

☐	knit
O	yo
/	k2tog
\	ssk
V	slip with yarn

WRITTEN INSTRUCTIONS

ADULT SMALL

Round 1: K3, k2tog, yo, k1, yo, ssk, k5, k2tog, yo, k1, yo, ssk, k2.

Round 2: K5, sl, k9, sl, k4.

Rounds 3 and 4: Repeat Rounds 1 and 2.

Rounds 5 and 6: Knit.

Round 7: K8, k2tog, yo, k1, yo, ssk, k7.

Round 8: K10, sl, k9.

Rounds 9 and 10: Repeat Rounds 7 and 8.

Rounds 11 and 12: Knit.

ADULT MEDIUM

Round 1: K4, k2tog, yo, k1, yo, ssk, k5, k2tog, yo, k1, yo, ssk, k3.

Round 2: K6, sl, k9, sl, k5.

Rounds 3 and 4: Repeat Rounds 1 and 2.

Rounds 5 and 6: Knit.

Round 7: K9, k2tog, yo, k1, yo, ssk, k8.

Round 8: K11, sl, k10.

Rounds 9 and 10: Repeat Rounds 7 and 8.

Rounds 11 and 12: Knit.

ADULT LARGE

Round 1: K3, k2tog, yo, k1, yo, ssk, k5, k2tog, yo, k1, yo, ssk, k6.

Round 2: K5, (sl, k9), k5, (sl, 8).

Rounds 3 and 4: Repeat rounds 1 and 2.

Rounds 5 and 6: Knit.

Round 7: K8, k2tog, yo, k1, yo, ssk, k5, k2tog, yo, k1, yo, ssk, k1.

Round 8: K10, sl, k9, sl, k3.

Rounds 9 and 10: Repeat rounds 7 and 8.

Rounds 11 and 12: Knit.

CANDY MOUNTAIN

Are you ready to use up those mini skeins? With only three rows of colourwork this is the perfect beginner friendly colourwork project. Have fun mixing and matching your colours together; choose one or ten different contrast colours.

YOU WILL NEED

NEEDLES

Size 2.25mm (US 1), or size needed to obtain tension, for your preferred method of knitting in the round.

NOTIONS

- Darning needle

YARN

The sample was knitted using Tot le Matin TOT Sock Yarn (75% Merino, 25% Nylon) fingering weight, 100g (425m/464yds) in the following shades:

- MC: Cabernet (1 skein)
- CC1: Nude (20g skein)
- CC2: Lagon (20g skein)
- CC3: Gallery (20g skein)
- CC4: Tobasco (20g skein)
- CC5: Eucalyptus (20g skein)

SIZES

Adult Small (Adult Medium, Adult Large)

To fit a foot circumference of approximately 7 (8) (8½)in / 18 (20.5) (21.5)cm

TENSION (GAUGE)
unblocked

36 stitches and 40 rows measure 4 x 4in (10 x 10cm) over stocking (stockinette) stitch using 2.25mm needles

CUFF

Using the long tail cast on (or preferred method) CO 56 (64) (72) stitches join for working in the round taking care not to twist your stitches.

Magic Loop: Divide the stitches evenly between your two needles 28 (32) (36) sts on each needle.

DPNS: Divide the stitches evenly between your four needles 14 (16) (18) sts on each needle.

Rounds 1-12: *K2, p2; repeat from *.

Round 13: Knit all stitches.

LEG

Start the colourwork chart and repeat the 7 (8) (8) sts around the sock changing the colour of mini skein each time. You will be working the colourwork on both the front and the back of the leg.

Continue knitting with the chart until you've reached the desired length from your cast-on edge. The sample was knitted to 5½in (14cm) from the ribbing for the size Adult Small, ending on Round 10.

HEEL

The short row heel is worked on half of your stitches with your MC.

Knit across the first 28 (32) (34) sts separating the stitches into three equal parts using stitch markers. If your stitch count isn't divisible by 3, then the middle section gets more stitches. (Eg; If it's 28, then divide it as 9 / 10 / 9). Turn work.

Row 1: (WS) Ds, purl to the end, turn work.

Row 2: (RS) Ds, knit to the last ds but do not work it, turn work.

Row 3: Ds, purl to the last ds but do not work it, turn work.

Repeat Row 2 and 3 until you have worked all the stitches on each side of the stitch markers.

You have now completed the first half of the short row heel. In this section as you come to a ds you will knit or purl it together treating it as a single stitch. (Note; Depending on your stitch count if you finish on a knit round start on Row 2 instead of Row 1).

Row 1: (RS) Knit to the first ds, knit the ds together as one st, turn work.

Row 2: (WS) Ds, purl to the first ds, purl the ds together as one st, turn work.

Row 3: Ds, knit to the first ds, knit it together as one st, repeat with the next ds, turn work.

Row 4: Ds, purl to the first ds, purl it together as one st, repeat with the next ds, turn work.

Repeat Rows 3 and 4 until you have worked all the stitches.

You are now ready to work in the round again. As your last row will be a WS row, knit one more round knitting all the ds together as you come to them.

I recommend on the following two rounds to pick up an extra stitch or two in between the heel gaps. This will help close any holes that were created. Pick up the stitches between the gap and knit them together with the first stitch on your needle.

PRO TIP: *If you're new to colourwork, try on the sock as you go to see how your tension is doing. If it's too tight you may need to go up a needle size.*

FOOT

You will continue working the colourwork chart starting at Round 1 until you've reached 1½ (1¾) (2)in / 4 (4.5) (5)cm shorter than your foot length ending on Round 10.

TOE

Round 1: K1, ssk, knit to the last 3 sts of section, k2tog, k1 (Repeat on both sections).

Round 2: Knit all stitches.

Magic Loop: Continue these two rounds until there are 12 (12) (16) sts left on each needle.

DPNS: Continue these two rounds until there are 6 (6) (8) sts left on each needle.

Graft together using the Kitchener stitch and weave in all ends. Block as desired.

If you want a bit more variety, you can switch up the order of CCs on the second sock.

CHARTS

Each square represents a stitch. Read all rows from right to left. Carry the unused strands of yarn across the WS of the work, twisting yarn after every three or four stitches to avoid long loops of yarn on the WS.

SMALL

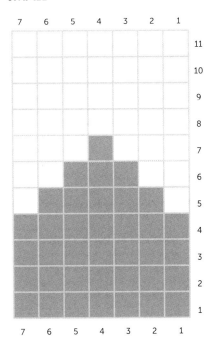

MEDIUM/LARGE

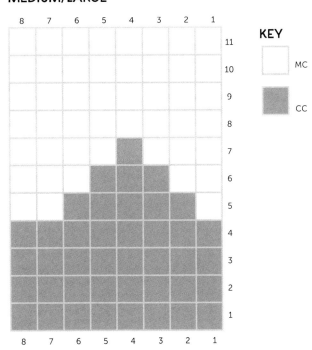

KEY

MC

CC

AUTUMN LOVe

Autumn Love socks are inspired by the hat I made using the same design. I just fell in love with the colourwork chart and knew it needed to become a fun pair of socks. Using three different contrast colours it's a perfect stash buster for any leftover yarns. Get ready to snuggle up and stay warm with these socks. They are knit cuff down with a heel flap and gusset.

YOU WILL NEED

NEEDLES
Size 2.25mm (US 1), or size needed to obtain tension, for your preferred method of knitting in the round.

OTHER TOOLS AND MATERIALS
• Darning needle

YARN
The sample was knitted using Tot le Matin TOT Sock Yarn (75% Merino, 25% Nylon), fingering, 100g (425m/464yds) in OOAK Sock Set:

• 100g and 3 x 20g mini skeins

SIZES
Adult Small/Medium (Adult Large)

To fit a foot circumference of approximately: 7 (8)in / 18 (20.5)cm

TENSION (GAUGE)
unblocked

36 stitches and 40 rows measure 4 x 4in (10 x 10cm) over stocking (stockinette) stitch using 2.25mm needles

PATTERN

CUFF

Using the long tail cast on (or preferred method) CO 64 (72) sts. Join for working in the round taking care not to twist your stitches.

Magic Loop: Divide the stitches evenly between your two needles 30 (36) sts on each needle.

DPNS: Divide the stitches evenly between your four needles 15 (18) sts on each needle.

Rounds 1-20: *K2, p2; repeat from *.

LEG

Start the colourwork chart and repeat the 8 sts around the sock. Please note: only work the 30 rounds of the chart once. Once completed, cut the CC and knit the rest with the MC.

Continue the sock in stocking stitch until desired length; sample was knitted to 6in (15cm) from the ribbing.

HEEL

The heel is worked over the first 32 (36) sts.

Row 1 (RS): *Sl1, k1; repeat from *, turn.

Row 2 (WS): Sl1, purl to end, turn.

Repeat these two rows a total of 15 times (30 rows).

HEEL TURN

Row 1 (RS): Sl1, k16 (18), ssk, k1, turn.

Row 2 (WS): Sl1, p5, p2tog, p1, turn.

Row 3: Sl1, knit to one st before gap, ssk, k1, turn.

Row 4: Sl1, purl to one st before gap, p2tog, p1, turn.

Repeat Rows 3 and 4 until all stitches have been worked.

Knit across heel stitches then pick up and knit 15 gusset sts along the edge of heel flap. Pick up an extra stitch on the ladder between the stitches on the row below to close any gaps bringing the total number of stitches picked up to 16. Knit across instep stitches. Pick up an extra stitch in the ladder between the stitches on the row below (to avoid a hole). Pick up 15 sts along the second side of heel flap.

GUSSET

When decreasing gusset stitches, only work decreases on Section 1 or the back of heel. This is the Section used to pick up all the gusset stitches. During these rounds make sure to knit all stitches on Section 2 (top of foot) without decreasing across the top of foot.

Round 1:

Section 1: K1, ssk, knit to 3 sts before the end of row, k2tog, k1.

Section 2: Knit all stitches.

Round 2:

Section 1 and 2: Knit all stitches.

Repeat these two rounds until work returns to the original stitch count of 64 (72).

Continue in stocking stitch until the work measures 1½ (1¾)in / 4 (4.5)cm shorter than the total foot length or desired negative ease.

TOE

Round 1: K1, ssk, knit to the last 3 sts, k2tog, k1 (Repeat on both needles).

Round 2: Knit.

Magic Loop: Continue these two rounds until there are 10 (12) sts left on each needle.

DPNS: Continue these two rounds until there are 5 (6) sts left on each needle.

Graft together using the Kitchener stitch and weave in all ends. Block as desired.

CHART

Each square represents a stitch. Read all rows from right to left
Carry the unused strands of yarn across the WS of the work,
twisting yarn after every three or four stitches to avoid long
loops of yarn on the WS.

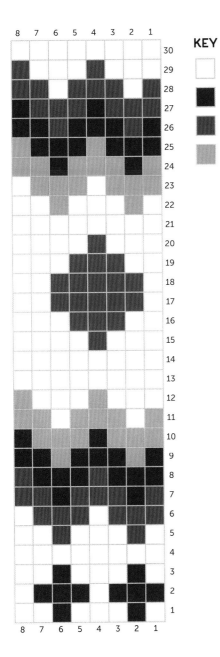

KEY

☐ MC

■ CC1

■ CC2

■ CC3

SNOWFLAKE DREAMS

Have you been wanting to knit the perfect colourwork pair of socks? Look no further, Snowflake Dreams is knit using only two colours for the whole sock making this the perfect introduction to a more advanced colourwork technique.

YOU WILL NEED

NEEDLES

Different sizes are made using the same number of stitches but different size needles.

- Small/Medium:

Size 2.5mm (US 1 to 2), or size needed to obtain tension, for your preferred method of knitting in the round.

- Medium/Large:

Size 2.75mm to 3mm (US 2 to 3), or size needed to obtain tension, for your preferred method of knitting in the round.

OTHER TOOLS AND MATERIALS

- Darning needle

YARN

The sample was knitted using Craftnut Yarns Platinum Sock (75% Superwash Merino, 25% Nylon), fingering weight, 100g (423m/463yds) in the following shades:

- MC: Night Sky (100g)
- CC: Bare (50g)

SIZES

Small/Medium (Medium/Large)

To fit a foot circumference of approximately 8 (9)in / 20.5 (23)cm

TENSION (GAUGE)

unblocked

Size Small/Medium: 34 stitches and 36 rows measure 4 x 4in (10 x 10cm) over stocking (stockinette) stitch using 2.25mm needles.

Size Medium/Large: 32 stitches and 34 rows measure 14 x 4in (10 x 10cm) over stocking (stockinette) stitch using 2.75mm needles

PATTERN

CUFF

Using the long tail cast on (or preferred method) CO 72 sts with your MC. Join for working in the round taking care not to twist your stitches.

Magic Loop: Divide the stitches evenly between your two needles, 36 sts on each needle.

DPNS: Divide the stitches evenly between your four needles, 18 sts on each needle.

Rounds 1-20: *K2, p2; repeat from *.

LEG

Using the charts, you'll be completing Chart A once on the front of your leg. For the back of the leg you'll be repeating Chart B six times.

Repeat Chart A and B until you've reached approximately 6½in (16.5cm) from your cast-on edge or desired length.

HEEL

The heel is completed in your MC.

The short row heel is worked on half of your stitches.

Knit across the first 36 sts separating the stitches into three equal parts using stitch markers. Turn work.

Row 1 (WS): Ds, purl to the end, turn work.

Row 2 (RS): Ds, knit to the last ds but do not work it, turn work.

Row 3: Ds, purl to the last ds but do not work it, turn work.

Repeat Rows 2 and 3 until you have worked all the stitches on each side of the stitch markers.

You have now completed the first half of the short row heel. In this section as you come to a ds you will knit or purl it together treating it as a single stitch. (Note; Depending on your stitch count if you finish on a knit round start on Row 2 instead of Row 1).

Row 1 (RS): Knit to the first ds, knit the ds together as one st, turn work.

Row 2 (WS): Ds, purl to the first ds, purl the ds together as one st, turn work.

Row 3: Ds, knit to the first ds, knit it together as one st, repeat with the next ds, turn work.

Row 4: Ds, purl to the first ds, purl it together as one st, repeat with the next ds, turn work.

Repeat Rows 3 and 4 until you have worked all the stitches.

You are now ready to work in the round again. As your last row will be a WS row, knit one more round knitting all the ds together as you come to them.

I recommend on the following two rounds to pick up an extra stitch or two in between the heel gaps. This will help close any holes that were created. Pick up the stitches between the gap and knit them together with the first stitch on your needle.

FOOT

Using the chart instructions you'll be completing Chart A once on the front of your leg. For the back of the leg you'll be repeating Chart B six times.

Repeat Chart A and B until you've reached 2in (5cm) shorter than your total foot length.

TOE

The toe is completed in your MC, you can cut your CC.

Round 1: K1, ssk, knit to the last 3 sts, k2tog, k1 (Repeat on both needles).

Round 2: Knit all stitches.

Magic Loop: Continue these two rounds until there are 12 sts left on each needle.

DPNS: Continue these two rounds until there are 6 sts left on each needle.

Graft together using the Kitchener stitch and weave in all ends. Block as desired.

CHARTS

Each square represents a stitch. Read all rows from right to left.
Carry the unused strands of yarn across the WS of the work,
twisting yarn after every three or four stitches to avoid long loops
of yarn on the WS.

CHART A

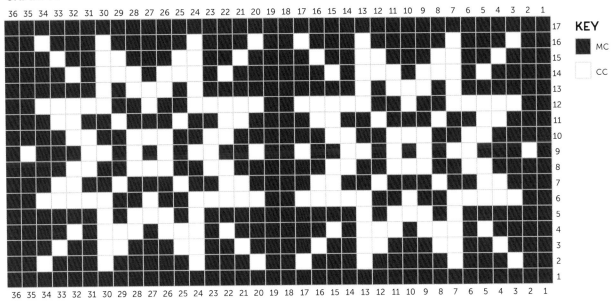

KEY

■ MC

□ CC

CHART B

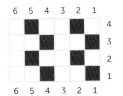

*Worked in different colours,
snowflakes can look a lot like flowers.
Using green and pink yarn could
make this a fun spring sock.*

DK SCRAPPY

It's no secret I LOVE DK weight socks; they are squishy and fast to knit. With most other sock patterns we always seem to have yarn leftover. I wanted to design a DK weight pair of socks to use up ALL your leftovers. Use this pattern either with DK weight yarns or use up fingering weight yarns held double. Have fun with this scrappy sock recipe!

YOU WILL NEED

NEEDLES
Size 3.25mm (US 3), or size needed to obtain tension, for your preferred method of knitting in the round.

NOTIONS
• Tapestry Needle

YARN
The sample was knitted using Lolodidit USA DK (100% Superwash Merino Wool), double knitting, 28g mini skein (64m/70yds) in the following shades:

• C1 Anduin (1 skein)

• C2 Stay Golden (1 skein)

• C3 Something Fall (1 skein)

• C4 Sh Boom (1 skein)

• C5 Dubble Bubble (1 skein)

SIZES
Toddler (Child) (Adult Small) (Adult Medium) (Adult Large)

To fit a foot circumference of approximately 6 (6½) (7) (8) (8½)in / 15 (16.5) (18) (20.5) (21.5)cm

TENSION (GAUGE)
unblocked

24 stitches and 36 rows measure 4 x 4in (10 x 10cm) over stocking (stockinette) stitch using 3.25mm needles

PATTERN

HOW TO CHOOSE YOUR COLOURS

Have fun with your colours, go with a certain colour theme or change it up using all those extra left-over yarns. Just make sure you check the yardage for the mini skeins with the required amount for the size you've chosen. Use anything between 1 or 10 different colours - make these socks your own.

Certain dyers also sell fun mini skein kits. If you're unsure about what colours to use, let them make the decision for you.

CALCULATING HOW LONG TO MAKE THE REPEATS

For this sock pattern each repeat took 4g of yarn, which is 8 rounds of stocking stitch (double check to see if your tension matches mine).

CUFF

Using the long tail cast on (or preferred method) and C1 CO 36 (40) (44) (48) (52) sts. Join for working in the round taking care not to twist your stitches.

Magic Loop: Divide the stitches evenly between your two needles 18 (20) (22) (24) (26) sts on each needle.

DPNS: Divide the stitches evenly between your four needles 9 (10) (11) (12) (13) sts on each needle.

Rounds 1-8: *K2, p2; repeat from *.

Cut C1, and continue with C2.

Round 9: Knit all stitches.

Rounds 10-16: *K2, p2; repeat from *.

Cut C2.

LEG

You will be knitting 8 rounds per colour for the whole sock cutting each colour after the repeat.

Rounds 1-8: Knit all stitches with C3.

Rounds 9-16: Knit all stitches with C4.

Rounds 17-24: Knit all stitches with C5.

Rounds 25-32: Knit all stitches with C1.

Rounds 33-40: Knit all stitches with C2.

Repeat Rounds 1-40 until you've reached the desired length from your cast-on edge. Ending after a full colour repeat. The sample was knitted to 5½in (14cm) from the cast-on edge for the size Adult Small.

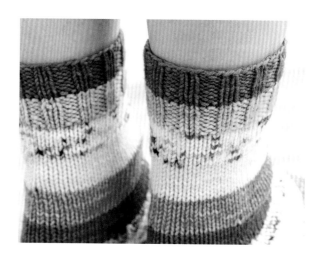

HEEL

The short row heel is worked on half of your stitches.

Using the next colour in the pattern. Knit across the first 18 (20) (22) (24) (26) sts separating the stitches into three equal parts using stitch markers. If your stitch count isn't divisible by 3, then the middle section gets more stitches. (Eg; If it's 20, then divide it as 6 / 8 / 6). Turn work.

Row 1 (WS): Ds, purl to the end, turn work.

Row 2: Ds, knit to the last ds but do not work it, turn work.

Row 3: Ds, purl to the last ds but do not work it, turn work.

Repeat Rows 2 and 3 until you have worked all the stitches on each side of the stitch markers.

You have now completed the first half of the short row heel. In this section as you come to a ds you will knit or purl it together treating it as a single stitch. (Note; Depending on your stitch count if you finish on a knit round start on Row 2 instead of Row 1).

Row 1 (RS): Knit to the first ds, knit the ds together as one st, turn work.

Row 2 (WS): Ds, purl to the first ds, purl the ds together as one st, turn work.

Row 3: Ds, knit to the first ds, knit it together as one st, repeat with the next ds, turn work.

Row 4: Ds, purl to the first ds, purl it together as one st, repeat with the next ds, turn work.

Repeat Rows 3 and 4 until you have worked all the stitches.

You are now ready to work in the round again. As your last row will be a WS row, knit one more round knitting all the ds together as you come to them. Knit the last round

I recommend on the following two rounds to pick up an extra stitch or two in between the heel gaps. This will help close any holes that were created. Pick up the stitches between the gap and knit them together with the first stitch on your needle.

Continue knitting in pattern until you've reached 1 (1½) (2) (2) (2¼)in / 2.5 (4) (5) (5) (5.5)cm shorter than your foot length ending after a full colour repeat.

TOE

Toe will be completed in the next CC in the pattern.

Round 1: K1, ssk, knit to the last 3 sts, k2tog, k1 (Repeat on both needles).

Round 2: Knit all stitches.

Magic Loop: Continue these two rounds until there are 8 (8) (10) (10) (10) sts left on each needle.

DPNS: Continue these two rounds until there are 4 (4) (5) (5) (5) sts left on each needle.

Graft together using the Kitchener stitch and weave in all ends. Block as desired.

Measure twice, knit once!

SCRAPPY FADED

Raise your hand if you have tons of leftover fingering weight yarn? Are you ready to use up all those scraps and leftovers to make a unique pair of socks? I've done all the work for you; all you have to do is choose your incredible colours and get knitting. You can choose a specific colour scheme, colour gradient or even do a full rainbow of colour. These socks are knit cuff down with a garter short row heel.

YOU WILL NEED

NEEDLES
Size 3.5mm (US 4), or size needed to obtain tension, for your preferred method of knitting in the round.

OTHER TOOLS AND MATERIALS
- Darning needle

YARN
The sample was knitted using fingering weight leftover yarns from my stash in the following colourways:

- C1: Sweet Skein O' Mine in Hygge
- C2: Pineapple Yarns in Seagull Attack
- C3: A Homespun House in Folklore
- C4: Hedgehog Fibres in Rose Hip
- C5: Sweet Skein O' Mine in Day Dreamer

SIZES
Toddler (Child) (Adult Small) (Adult Medium) (Adult Large) (Adult X-Large)

To fit a foot circumference of approximately: 5½ (6½) (7) (8) (8½) (9½)in / 14 (16.5) (18) (20.5) (21.5) (24)cm

TENSION (GAUGE)
unblocked

26 stitches and 32 rows measure 4 x 4in (10 x 10cm) over stocking (stockinette) stitch using 3.5mm needles

PATTERN

CALCULATING HOW LONG TO MAKE THE REPEATS

You will need to calculate how long your desired leg length will be and your total foot length. You will add these numbers together and divide it by 9. This is the length of each repeat.

CUFF

Holding the C1 yarn double, using the long tail cast on (or preferred method) CO 36 (40) (44) (48) (52) (60) sts. Join for working in the round taking care not to twist your stitches.

Magic Loop: Divide the stitches evenly between your two needles 18 (20) (22) (24) (26) (30) sts on each needle.

DPNS: Divide the stitches evenly between your four needles 9 (10) (11) (12) (13) (15) sts on each needle.

Rounds 1-10: *K2, P2; repeat from *.

Drop 1 strand of your C1 and add 1 strand of C2.

LEG

Continue knitting in stocking stitch in pattern until you've reached your desired leg length. The sample was knitted to 4½in (11.5cm) from the ribbing for the size Adult Small. Proceed to the heel with the two strands following your pattern repeat.

HEEL

The garter short row heel is worked on half of your stitches. Garter stitch is created when you knit on both the RS and WS of the work.

Knit across the first 18 (20) (22) (24) (26) (30) sts separating the stitches into three parts using stitch markers. If your stitch count isn't divisible by 3, then the middle section gets more stitches. (Eg; If it's 26, then divide it as 8 / 10 / 8) Turn work.

Row 1 (WS): Ds, knit to the end, turn work.

Row 2 (RS): Ds, knit to the last ds but do not work it, turn work.

Row 3: Ds, knit to the last ds but do not work it, turn work.

Repeat Rows 2 and 3 until you have worked all the sts on each side of the stitch markers.

You have now completed the first half of the short row heel. In this section as you come to a ds you will knit it together treating it as a single stitch. (Note; Depending on your stitch count if you finish on a WS start on Row 2 instead of Row 1)

Row 1 (RS): Knit to the first ds, knit the ds together as one st, turn work.

Row 2 (WS): Ds, knit to the first ds, purl the ds together as one st, turn work.

Row 3: Ds, knit to the first ds, knit it together as one st, repeat with the next ds, turn work.

Row 4: Ds, knit to the first ds, purl it together as one st, repeat with the next ds, turn work.

Repeat Rows 3 and 4 until you have worked all the stitches.

You are now ready to work in the round again. As your last row will be a WS row, knit one more round knitting all the ds together as you come to them.

I recommend on the following two rounds to pick up an extra stitch or two in between the heel gaps. This will help close any holes that were created. Pick up the stitches between the gap and knit them together with the first stitch on your needle.

Continue knitting in pattern until you've reached 1 (1½) (2) (2) (2¼in) / 2.5 (4) (5) (5) (5.5)cm shorter than your foot length. Proceed to the toe in your two strands, following your pattern repeat.

Making socks out of scraps of yarn is a great way of reducing waste. I save all my yarn leftovers until I have enough for these socks.

TOE

Round 1: K1, ssk, knit to the last 3 sts, k2tog, k1 (Repeat on both needles).

Round 2: Knit all stitches.

Magic Loop: Continue these two rounds until there are 8 (8) (10) (10) (10) sts left on each needle.

DPNS: Continue these two rounds until there are 4 (4) (5) (5) (5) sts left on each needle.

Graft together using the Kitchener stitch and weave in all ends. Block as desired.

PATTERN REPEAT

- C1 held double
- Drop 1 strand of C1, and add 1 strand of C2
- C1 and C2 held double
- Drop 1 strand of C1 and add 1 strand of C2
- C2 held double
- Drop 1 strand of C2 and add 1 strand of C3
- C2 and C3 held double
- Drop 1 strand of C2 and add 1 strand of C3
- C3 held double
- Drop 1 strand of C3 and add 1 strand of C4
- C3 and C4 held double
- Drop 1 strand of C3 and add 1 strand of C4
- C4 held double
- Drop 1 strand of C4 and add 1 strand of C5
- C4 and C5 held double
- Drop 1 strand of C4 and add 1 strand of C5
- C5 held double

STRIPES GONE WILD

There's something about stripes that make your knitting project go faster. Create your own fun pattern with these stripe socks, which are designed for you to have fun with colour – choose one or ten different colour strips to make them your own. This pattern comes sized for the whole family, so enjoy making these over and over again. This pair of socks is designed toe up with an afterthought heel.

YOU WILL NEED

NEEDLES
Size 2.25mm (US 1), or size needed to obtain tension, for your preferred method of knitting in the round.

OTHER TOOLS AND MATERIALS
• Darning needle
• Waste yarn (optional for heel)

YARN
The sample was knitted using A Homespun House Soft Sock (75% Superwash Merino, 25% Nylon) fingering weight, 100g (370m/407yds) in the following shades:

• MC: Flash Dance (1 ball)
• C1: Barbie (Pink) (20g)
• C2: Refresh (Green) (20g)
• C3: Electric Feel (Yellow) (20g)
• C4: Purple People Eater (Purple) (20g)
• C5: Ditzy (Blue) (20g)

SIZES
Toddler (Child) (Adult Small) (Adult Medium) (Adult Large)

To fit a foot circumference of approximately: 4-5 (5-6) (6½) (7) (8)in / 10-13 (13-15) (16.5) (18) (20.5)cm

TENSION (GAUGE)
unblocked

36 stitches and 40 rows measure 4 x 4in (10 x 10cm) over stocking (stockinette) stitch using 2.25mm needles

PATTERN

TOE

Using the Turkish cast on (or preferred method) and your MC, CO 16 (18) (20) (24) (28) sts: 8 (9) (10) (12) (14) sts each on the top and bottom needles.

Round 1: Knit all stitches.

Round 2: *K1, kfb, knit to the last two sts on needle, kfb, k1; repeat from * on the second needle.

Repeat these two rounds until you've reached 40 (48) (56) (64) (72) total sts: 20 (24) (28) (32) (36) sts each on the top and bottom needles.

Magic Loop: Divide the stitches evenly between your two needles 20 (24) (28) (32) (36) sts on each needle.

DPNS: Divide the stitches evenly between your four needles 10 (12) (14) (16) (18) sts on each needle.

FOOT

Rounds 1-8: Knit with your MC.

Rounds 9-12: Knit with your CC.

Knit in pattern changing your CC each time, until you've reached the required foot length. Place removable stitch marker or use waste yarn to mark location for heel.

Using waste yarn:

K20 (24) (28) (32) (36) sts using waste yarn in a contrast colour to your MC. Transfer those 20 (24) (28) (32) (36) sts back onto the left needle. K20 (24) (28) (32) (36) sts in your MC.

Work in stocking stitch, knitting every round until you have reached your desired leg length, measured from the removable heel marker or waste yarn. You will cut in your heel after finishing the cuff.

LEG

Continue knitting in pattern changing your CC each time.

The sample was knitted to 6in (15cm) from the waste yarn before placing the cuff in the size, Adult small.

CUFF

The cuff is completed in your MC.

TODDLER AND CHILD SIZES

Rounds 1-6: *K2, p2; repeat from *.

ADULT SIZES

Rounds 1-8: *K2, p2; repeat from *.

When choosing sock yarn, make sure to choose something that has at least 10-15% Nylon. This will help with the durability of the socks.

HEEL

The heel is completed in both your MC and a CC.

Now that you've finished your cuff, return to the place where you put your waste yarn. Pick up 20 (24) (28) (32) (36) sts each on rows below and above the contrast waste yarn. You will have 40 (48) (56) (64) (72) sts total for the heel. Remove the contrast waste yarn by picking out each stitch.

Cut the right leg of a stitch in the middle of the row in between your two needles. You will carefully remove the stitches on that row except the last two sts on each side. Do not cut this yarn, you will use it to weave in any holes/ends later. Join your working yarn, use the tail to visually mark where your beginning of round is.

Round 1: *K1, ssk, knit to the last 3 sts on first needle, k2tog, k1; repeat from * on the second needle.

Round 2: Knit all stitches.

Magic Loop: Continue these two rounds until there are 20 (20) (22) (22) (22) sts left on each needle.

DPNS: Continue these two rounds until there are 10 (10) (11) (11) (11) sts left on each needle.

Cut your MC and switch to a CC of your choice.

Magic Loop: Continue these two rounds until there are 10 (10) (12) (12) (12) sts left on each needle.

DPNS: Continue these two rounds until there are 5 (5) (6) (6) (6) sts left on each needle.

Cut the yarn leaving a 12in (30.5cm) tail and use the Kitchener stitch to graft the heel closed.

Weave in all your ends and do a happy dance! You finished a sock!

> **PRO TIP:** *Do you have issues with ladders on the side of your sock? Try pulling tighter on the last three stitches and the first three stitches on the next needle.*

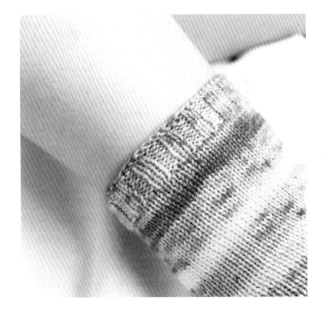

GET YOUR FADE ON

This pair of socks was designed with a fun faded 50g skein set. Have fun making up your own fade or let a yarn dyer do the work for you. You can purchase fade sets from multiple different yarn dyers. This pattern is designed cuff down and is sized for the whole family. It features a German short row heel.

YOU WILL NEED

NEEDLES
Size 3.5mm (US 4), or size needed to obtain tension, for your preferred method of knitting in the round.

OTHER TOOLS AND MATERIALS
• Darning needle

YARN
The sample was knitted using The Creative Knitter Sock (75% Superwash Merino, 25% Nylon), fingering weight, 50g (210m/230yds) in Beach Games Fade Bundle.

• C1: Cream
• C2: Cream with light blue
• C3: Light blue and dark blue
• C4: Dark blue

SIZES
Toddler (Child) (Adult Small) (Adult Medium) (Adult Large) (Adult X-Large)

To fit a foot circumference of approximately 5½ (6½) (7) (8) (8½) (9½) in / 14 (16.5) (18) (20.5) (21.5) (24)cm

TENSION (GAUGE)
unblocked

22 stitches and 32 rows measure 4 x 4in (10 x 10cm) over stocking (stockinette) stitch using 3.5mm needles

PATTERN

ABOUT THE PATTERN

This is the time to get your fade on! Use up those gorgeous 50g skeins of yarn to create a beautiful faded pair of socks.

Here are some tips to keep in mind when you're knitting these for the first time

- Check your tension, all fingering weight yarns have different thickness and sizes. Some can be on the thinner side or thicker.

- Notes on tension; if you have too many stitches you need to go up a needle size. If you don't have enough stitches you need to go down a size needle.

- Don't want to knit double stranded? No worries you can use any worsted weight yarn instead.

- This would be an amazing project for using up any mini skeins! Pick a colour for your base and change up the mini skeins every 6-8 rounds to create an amazing marled unique pair of socks.

- How to calculate the colour repeats: For the length of each colour repeat: Measure your total foot length plus your desired leg length and divide it by the number of colours you have. This will determine how long each repeat will be in the sock.

CUFF

Holding the C1 yarn double, using the long tail cast on (or preferred method) CO 32 (36) (40) (44) (48) (52) sts. Join for working in the round taking care not to twist your stitches.

Magic Loop: Divide the stitches evenly between your two needles 30 (36) sts on each needle.

DPNS: Divide the stitches evenly between your four needles 15 (18) sts on each needle.

Rounds 1-10: *K2, p2; repeat from *.

Cut your C1 and switch to C2.

LEG

Continue knitting in stocking stitch until you've reached the calculated length of repeat (see About the Pattern) from your colour change. Cut your C2 and switch to C3.

Continue knitting in stocking stitch until you've reached desired leg length. The sample was knitted to 5½in (14cm) from the ribbing for the size Adult Small. Proceed to the heel with your C3.

HEEL

The short row heel is worked on half of your stitches.

Knit across the first 16 (18) (20) (22) (24) sts separating the stitches into three equal parts using stitch markers. If your stitch count isn't divisible by 3, then the middle section gets more stitches (Ex; If it's 20, then divide it as 6 / 8 / 6). Turn work.

Row 1 (WS): Ds, purl to the end, turn work.

Row 2 (RS): Ds, knit to the last ds but do not work it, turn work.

Row 3: Ds, purl to the last ds but do not work it, turn work.

Repeat Rows 2 and 3 until you have worked all the stitches on each side of the stitch markers.

You have now completed the first half of the short row heel. In this section as you come to a ds you will knit or purl it together treating it as a single stitch. (Note; Depending on your stitch count if you finish on a knit round start on Row 2 instead of Row 1).

Row 1 (RS): Knit to the first ds, knit the ds together as one st, turn work.

Row 2 (WS): Ds, purl to the first ds, purl the ds together as one st, turn work.

Row 3: Ds, knit to the first ds, knit it together as one st, repeat with the next ds, turn work.

Row 4: Ds, purl to the first ds, purl it together as one st, repeat with the next ds, turn work.

Repeat Rows 3 and 4 until you have worked all the stitches.

You are now ready to work in the round again. As your last row will be a WS row, knit one more round knitting all the ds stitches together as you come to them.

I recommend on the following two rounds to pick up an extra stitch or two in between the heel gaps. This will help close any holes that were created. Pick up the stitches between the gap and knit them together with the first stitch on your needle.

Continue knitting in stocking stitch until you've reached the calculated length of repeat. Cut your C3 and switch to C4.

Continue knitting in pattern until you've reached 1 (1½) (2) (2) (2¼)in / 2.5 (4) (5) (5) (5.5)cm shorter than your foot length. Proceed to the toe in your C4.

TOE

Round 1: K2, ssk, knit to the last 4 sts, k2tog, k2 (Repeat on both needles).

Round 2: Knit all stitches.

Magic Loop: Continue these two rounds until there are 8 (8, 10, 10, 10) sts left on each needle.

DPNS: Continue these two rounds until there are 4 (4, 5, 5, 5) sts left on each needle.

Graft together using the Kitchener stitch and weave in all ends. Block as desired.

Work the fade in the opposite direction starting with the darker colour to make a fun mismatched pair of socks.

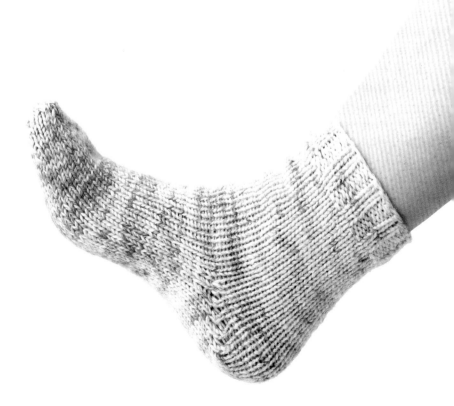

GINGERBREAD LATTE

It's no secret how much I love a good latte! There's something very magical about the warm spices of the holiday season with some foamed milk. This pattern is one of my favourites of the designs I've created over the years. The cables and twisted stitches create such an elegant design while still being a very simple five-row repeat. Enjoy knitting this pair of socks while sipping on your own latte.

YOU WILL NEED

NEEDLES
Size 2.25mm (US 1), or size needed to obtain tension, for your preferred method of knitting in the round.

OTHER TOOLS AND MATERIALS
• Darning needle

YARN
The sample was knitted using Lizzie Anne Yarns in Soft Sock (75% Wool, 25% Nylon) fingering weight, 100g (425m/465yds) in Gingerbread Latte Sock Set.

• 100g and a 20g mini skein

SIZES
Adult Small (Adult Medium) (Adult Large)

To fit a foot circumference of approximately 7 (8) (8½)in / 18 (20.5) (21.5)cm

TENSION (GAUGE)
unblocked

34 stitches and 48 rows measure 4 x 4in (10 x 10cm) over stocking (stockinette) stitch using 2.25mm needles

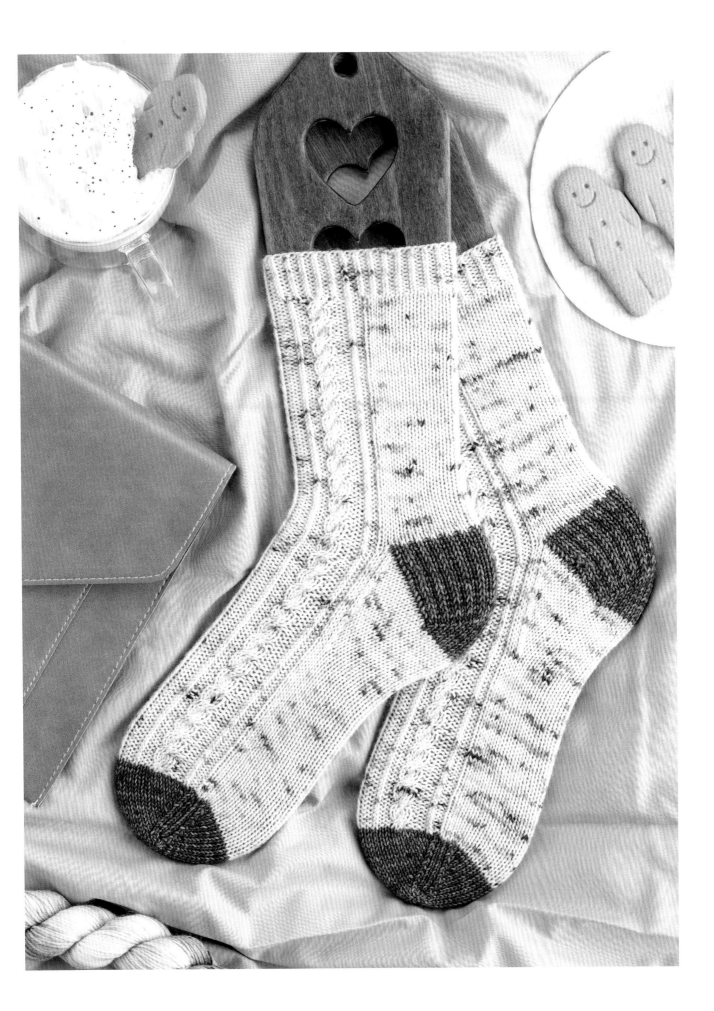

PATTERN

CUFF

Using the long tail cast on (or preferred method) CO 56 (64) (72) sts. Join for working in the round taking care not to twist your stitches.

Magic Loop: Divide the stitches evenly between your two needles 28 (32, 36) sts on each needle.

DPNS: Divide the stitches evenly between your four needles 14 (16, 18) sts on each needle.

Rounds 1-10: *K1tbl, p1; repeat from *.

LEG

The stitches will be divided between Section 1 and Section 2. Section 1 will be the front of your foot while Section 2 will be the back.

Use either the written or charted instructions for Section 1.

For Section 2: Knit all stitches.

Cut CC and knit the leg in MC.

Continue working in pattern until leg has reached the desired length ending with Round 5. The sample was knitted to 6in (15cm) from the ribbing.

HEEL

Heel is worked flat with your CC on Section 1 or half the stitches 28 (32, 36).

Row 1 (RS): *Sl1, k1; repeat from *, turn.

Row 2 (WS): Sl1, purl to end, turn.

Repeat these two rows a total of 15 (16) (16) times for a total of 30 (32) (32) rows.

HEEL TURN

Row 1 (RS): Sl1, k16 (18) (20), ssk, k, turn.

Row 2 (WS): Sl1, p5, p2tog, p1, turn.

Row 3: Sl1, knit to one st before gap, ssk, k1, turn.

Row 4: Sl1, purl to one st before gap, p2tog, p1, turn.

Repeat Rows 3 and 4 until all stitches have been worked. Cut your CC.

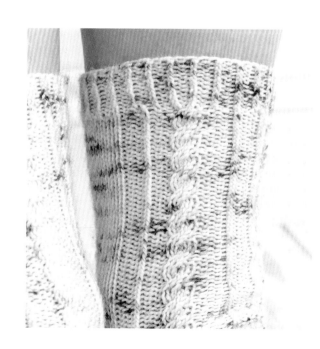

Using MC: Knit across remaining heel sts, pick up and knit 15 (16) (16) sts along the edge of heel flap. Pick up an extra stitch on the ladder between the stitches on the row below to close any gaps, bringing the total number of stitches picked up to 16 (17) (17). Knit across instep stitches. Pick up 16 (17, 17) sts on the other gusset side starting with the extra stitch on the ladder between the stitches on the row below to close any gaps.

GUSSET

When decreasing gusset stitches, only work decreases on Section 1 or back of heel. This is the needle (section) used to pick up all the gusset stitches. During these rounds make sure to knit all stitches on Section 2 (top of foot) without decreasing across the top of foot.

Round 1:

Section 1: K1, ssk, knit to 3 sts before the end of needle, k2tog, k1.

Section 2: Knit all stitches.

Round 2:

Section 1 and 2: Knit all stitches.

Continue Rounds 1 and 2 until work returns to the original stitch count of 56 (64) (72) sts.

Continue knitting in pattern for the front of the sock until the work measures 2 (2) (2½)in / 5 (5) (6.5)cm shorter than the total foot length or desired negative ease.

TOE

Round 1: K1, ssk, knit to the last 3 sts, k2tog, k1 (Repeat on both needles)

Round 2: Knit all stitches.

Magic Loop: Continue these two rounds until there are 8 (12) (12) sts left on each needle.

DPNS: Continue these two rounds until there are 4 (6) (6) sts left on each needle.

Graft together using the Kitchener stitch and weave in all ends. Block as desired.

Socks are a great way to try new techniques, like cables, texture or colourwork.

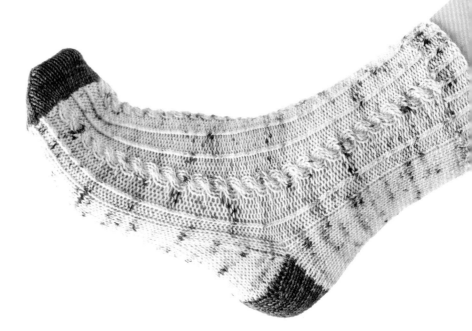

CHARTS

Each square represents a stitch. Read all rows from right to left.

SMALL

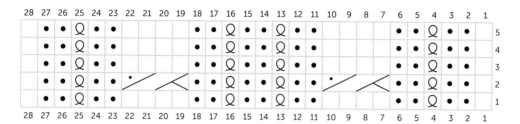

MEDIUM

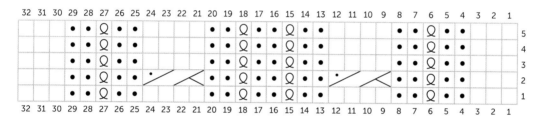

LARGE

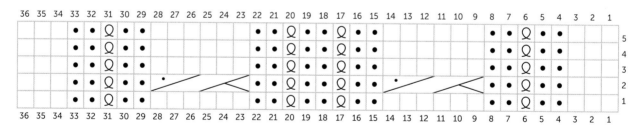

KEY

☐	knit
•	purl
Q	k
⟋⟍	2/2 RPC
⟋⟍	3/3 RPC

WRITTEN INSTRUCTIONS

SMALL

Round 1 and all odd-numbered rounds: K1, (p2, k1tbl, p2, k4, p2, k1tbl) x 2, p2, k1 .

Round 2: K1, (p2, k1tbl, p2, 2/2 RPC, p2, k1tbl) x 2, p2, k1.

Round 4: Repeat Round 1.

MEDIUM

Round 1 and all odd-numbered rounds: K3, (p2, k1tbl, p2, k4, p2, k1tbl) x 2, p2, k3.

Round 2: K3, (p2, k1tbl, p2, 2/2 RPC, p2, k1tbl) x 2, p2, k3.

Round 4: Repeat Round 1.

LARGE

Round 1 and all odd-numbered rounds: K3, (p2, k1tbl, p2, k6, p2, k1tbl) x 2, p2, k3.

Round 2: K3, (p2, k1tbl, p2, 3/3 RPC, p2, k1tbl) x 2, p2, k3.

Round 4: Repeat Round 1.

JUST ROLL WITH IT

I love a good sock set, but sometimes I don't want to use it for heels/toes and cuffs. I wanted to design this fun sock pattern as an alternative way to use up a sock set. For this pattern you'll need two mini skeins as the contrast colour. It features a rolled cuff which is playful and oh so simple to do, your children will LOVE these cute socks! The pattern is knit toe up with an afterthought heel.

YOU WILL NEED

NEEDLES
Size 2.25mm (US 1), or size needed to obtain tension, for your preferred method of knitting in the round.

OTHER TOOLS AND MATERIALS
• Darning needle

YARN
The sample was knitted using The Discrete Unicorn High Twist Sock (100% Superwash Merino), fingering weight, 100g (365m/399yds), 50g (183m/200yds) in the following shades:

• MC: 80's Christmas Tree (100g)

• C1: Electric (Blue) (20g)

• C2: Wizard (Purple) (20g)

SIZES
Toddler (Child) (Adult Small) (Adult Medium) (Adult Large)

To fit a foot circumference of approximately: 4-5 (5-6) (6½) (7) (8)in / 10-13 (13-15) (16.5) (18) (20.5)cm

TENSION (GAUGE)
unblocked

36 stitches and 40 rows measure 4 x 4in (10 x 10cm) over stocking (stockinette) stitch using 2.25mm needles

PATTERN

TOE

Using the Turkish cast on (or preferred method) and your MC, CO 16 (18) (20) (24) (28) sts: 8 (9) (10) (12) (14) sts each on the top and bottom needles.

Round 1: Knit all stitches.

Round 2: *K1, kfb, knit to the last two sts on needle, kfb, k1; repeat from * on the second needle.

Repeat these two rounds until you've reached 40 (48) (56) (64) (72) total sts: 20 (24) (28) (32) (36) sts each on the top and bottom needles.

Magic Loop: Divide the stitches evenly between your two needles 20 (24) (28) (32) (36) sts on each needle.

DPNS: Divide the stitches evenly between your four needles 10 (12) (14) (16) (18) sts on each needle.

FOOT

Work in stocking stitch, knitting every round until you've reached the required foot length. Place removable stitch marker or use waste yarn to mark location for heel.

Using waste yarn:

K20 (24) (28) (32) (36) sts using waste yarn in a contrast colour to your MC. Transfer those 20 (24) (28) (32) (36) sts back onto the left needle. K20 (24) (28) (32) (36) sts in your MC.

Work in stocking stitch, knitting every round until you have reached your desired leg length, measured from the removable heel marker or waste yarn. You will cut in your heel after finishing the cuff.

LEG

Work in stocking stitch, knitting every round until you have reached 1½in (4cm) from your heel.

Rounds 1-3: Knit all stitches with C1.

Rounds 4-9: Knit all stitches with MC.

Rounds 10-21: Knit all stitches with C2.

Rounds 22-27: Knit all stitches with MC.

Rounds 28-30: Knit all stitches with C1.

Rejoin MC.

Work in stocking stitch, knitting every round, until you have reached 2in (5cm) from the last C1 stripe.

Bind off all stitches using Jeny's Surprisingly Stretchy Cast (Bind) Off (see Techniques or use a stretchy bind off your choice) leaving a 12in (30.5cm) tail to weave in the end later.

PRO TIP: *If you don't like the look of a rolled cuff? Don't worry; you can add your favourite cuff method instead.*

HEEL

The heel is completed in your MC.

Now that you've finished your cuff, return to the place where you put your waste yarn. Pick-up 20 (24) (28) (32) (36) sts each on rows below and above the contrast waste yarn. You will have 40 (48) (56) (64) (72) sts total for the heel. Remove the contrast waste yarn by picking out each stitch.

Cut the right leg of a stitch in the middle of the row in between your two needles. You will carefully remove the stitches on that row except the last two stitches on each side. Do not cut this yarn, you will use it to weave in any holes/ends later. Join your working yarn, use the tail to visually mark where your beginning of round is.

Round 1: *K1, ssk, knit to the last 3 sts on first needle, k2tog, k1; repeat from * on the second needle.

Round 2: Knit all stitches.

Magic Loop: Continue these two rounds until there are 10 (10) (12) (12) (12) sts left on each needle.

DPNS: Continue these two rounds until there are 5 (5) (6) (6) (6) sts left on each needle.

Cut the yarn leaving a 11¾in (30cm) tail and use the Kitchener stitch to graft the heel closed.

Weave in all your ends and do a happy dance! You finished a sock!

Don't shy away from trying a new construction method like toe up or afterthought heels.

OTHER SIDE OF THE RAINBOW

This pattern is all about having fun with colour and is also great for using up all your leftover mini skeins. Choose a main colour and go crazy with the minis! Want to make them into full length socks? Keep on knitting the leg until you've reached your desired length then proceed to the cuff.

YOU WILL NEED

NEEDLES

Size 2.25mm (US 1), or size needed to obtain tension, for your preferred method of knitting in the round.

OTHER TOOLS AND MATERIALS

- Darning needle

YARN

The sample was knitted using Lolodidit Loriginal (85% Extra Fine Superwash Merino, 15% Nylon) fingering weight, 100g (402m/440yds)

MC: Folsom (1 skein)

Lolodidit Loriginal (85% Extra Fine Superwash Merino, 15% Nylon) fingering weight, 28g (113m/124yds) in the following shades:

- C1: Outrageous (red) (1 skein)
- C2: Big Girls Don't Cry (pink) (1 skein)
- C3: Violet Beauregarde (purple) (1 skein)
- C4: Moiraine (blue) (1 skein)
- C5: Elayne (green) (1 skein)
- C6: Oow I Feel Good (yellow) (1 skein)

SIZES

Toddler (Child) (Adult Small) (Medium) (Large)

To fit approx. a foot circumference of 4-5 (5-6) (6½) (7) (8) in / 10-13 (13-15) (16.5) (18) (20.5)cm

TENSION (GAUGE)
unblocked

36 stitches and 40 rows measure 4 x 4in (10 x 10cm) over stocking (stockinette) stitch using 2.25mm needles

TOE

Using the Turkish cast on (or preferred method) and your MC, CO 16 (18) (20) (24) (28) sts: 8 (9) (10) (12) (14) sts each on the top and bottom needles.

Round 1: Knit all stitches.

Round 2: *K1, kfb, knit to the last two sts on needle, kfb, k1; repeat from * on the second needle.

Repeat these two rounds until you've reached 40 (48) (56) (64) (72) total sts: 20 (24) (28) (32) (36) sts each on the top and bottom needles.

Magic Loop: Divide the stitches evenly between your two needles 20 (24) (28) (32) (36) sts on each needle.

DPNS: Divide the stitches evenly between your four needles 10 (12) (14) (16) (18) sts on each needle.

FOOT

Rounds 1-10: Knit with your CC.

Rounds 11 and 12: Knit with your MC.

Knit in pattern changing your CC each time, until you've reached the required foot length. Place removable stitch marker or use waste yarn to mark location for heel.

Using waste yarn:

K20 (24) (28) (32) (36) sts using waste yarn in a contrast colour to your MC. Transfer those 20 (24) (28) (32) (36) sts back onto the left needle. K20 (24) (28) (32) (36) sts in your MC.

Work in stocking stitch, knitting every round until you have reached your desired leg length, measured from the removable heel marker or waste yarn. You will cut in your heel after finishing the cuff.

LEG

Continue knitting in pattern changing your CC each time.

The sample was knitted to 1in (2.5cm) before placing the cuff.

Set up round: Cut your CC, and knit all stitches with your MC.

Cuff is completed in your MC.

TODDLER AND CHILD SIZES:

Rounds 1-8: *K2, p2; repeat from *.

ADULT SIZES

Rounds 1-10: *K2, p2; repeat from *.

HEEL

The heel is completed in your MC.

Now that you've finished your cuff, return to the place where you put your waste yarn. Pick up 20 (24) (28) (32) (36) sts each on rows below and above the contrast waste yarn. You will have 40 (48) (56) (64) (72) sts total for the heel. Remove the contrast waste yarn by picking out each stitch.

Cut the right leg of a stitch in the middle of the row in between your two needles. You will carefully remove the stitches on that row except the last two stitches on each side. Do not cut this yarn, you will use it to weave in any holes/ends later. Join your working yarn, use the tail to visually mark where your beginning of round is.

Round 1: *K1, ssk, knit to the last 3 sts on first needle, k2tog, k1; repeat from * on the second needle.

Round 2: Knit all stitches.

Magic Loop: Continue these two rounds until there are 10 (10) (12) (12) (12) sts left on each needle.

DPNS: Continue these two rounds until there are 5 (5) (6) (6) (6) sts left on each needle.

Cut the yarn leaving a 11¾in (30cm) tail and use the Kitchener stitch to graft the heel closed.

Weave in all your ends and do a happy dance! You finished a sock!

> **PRO TIP:** *If you don't like shorty socks, feel free to add length to the leg by repeating the colours or continuing with your MC.*

WARM WOOLLY HUGS

Do you need a warm pair of socks that you can knit up in a few days? These bulky weight socks are perfect for snuggling up next to a warm fireplace (and your knitting). I've graded these for the whole family giving you the opportunity to make them for the holiday season! Quick gift knit? Yes please!!

YOU WILL NEED

NEEDLES
Size 3.25mm (US 3), or size needed to obtain tension, for your preferred method of knitting in the round.

OTHER TOOLS AND MATERIALS
• Darning needle

YARN
The sample was knitted using Knit Picks Wool of the Andes Bulky (100% Superwash Wool), bulky, 100g (125m/137yds) in the following shades:

• MC: Gosling (28214) (1 skein)

• CC: Cobblestone Heather (26503) (1 skein)

SIZES
Adult Small (Adult Medium) (Adult Large)

To fit a foot circumference of approximately 7 (8) (9½)in / 18 (20.5) (24)

TENSION (GAUGE)
unblocked

20 stitches and 24 rows measure 4 x 4in (10 x 10cm) over stocking (stockinette) stitch using 3.25mm needles

PATTERN

CUFF

Using the long tail cast on (or preferred method) CO 36 (40, 48) sts with your CC. Join for working in the round taking care not to twist your stitches.

Magic Loop: Divide the stitches evenly between your two needles 18 (20) (24) sts on each needle.

DPNS: Divide the stitches evenly between your four needles 9 (10) (12) sts on each needle.

Round 1: *K1, p1; repeat from *.

Repeat Round 1 until your work measures 3in (7.5cm) from the cast-on edge.

Cut your CC and switch to your MC.

LEG

Work in stocking stitch (knitting every round) for 1in (2.5cm) or until you've reached the desired length from your cast-on edge.

HEEL

The garter short row heel is worked on half of your stitches. Garter stitch is created when you knit on both the RS and WS of the work.

Knit across the first 18 (20) (24) sts separating the stitches into three equal parts using stitch markers. If your stitch count isn't divisible by 3, then the middle section gets more stitches. (Eg. If it's 20, then divide it as 6 / 8 / 6) Turn work.

Row 1 (WS): Ds, knit to the end, turn work.

Row 2 (RS): Ds, knit to the last ds but do not work it, turn work.

Row 3: Ds, knit to the last ds but do not work it, turn work.

Repeat Rows 2 and 3 until you have worked all the stitches on each side of the stitch markers.

You have now completed the first half of the short row heel. In this section as you come to a ds you will knit it together treating it as a single stitch. (Note; Depending on your stitch count if you finish on a WS start on Row 2 instead of Row 1).

Row 1 (RS): Knit to the first ds, knit the ds together as one st, turn work.

Row 2: Ds, knit to the first ds, purl the ds together as one st, turn work.

Row 3: Ds, knit to the first ds, knit it together as one st, repeat with the next ds stitch, turn work.

Row 4: Ds, knit to the first ds, purl it together as one st, repeat with the next ds stitch, turn work.

Repeat Rows 3 and 4 until you have worked all the stitches.

You are now ready to work in the round again. As your last row will be a WS row, knit one more round knitting all the ds stitches together as you come to them. Knit the last round.

I recommend on the following two rounds to pick up an extra stitch or two in between the heel gaps. This will help close any holes that were created. Pick up the stitches between the gap and knit them together with the first stitch on your needle.

Continue knitting in pattern until you've reached 2 (2) (2¼)in / 5 (5) (5.5)cm shorter than your foot length.

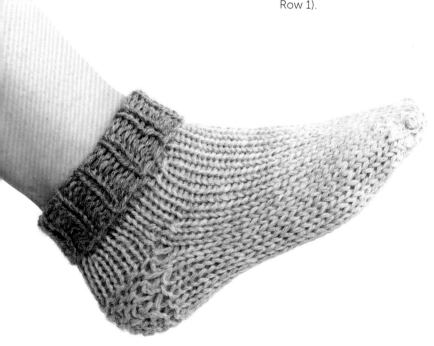

TOE

Round 1: K1, ssk, knit to the last 3 sts, k2tog, k1 (Repeat on both needles).

Round 2: Knit all stitches.

Magic Loop: Continue these two rounds until there are 8 (10) (10) sts left on each needle.

DPNS: Continue these two rounds until there are 4 (5) (5) sts left on each needle.

Graft together using the Kitchener stitch and weave in all ends. Block as desired.

For an extra cosy pair of socks, work a longer cuff. You'll need more CC but your ankles will stay nice and warm.

RAINBOW WAY

I love a simple colourwork pattern that looks more complicated than it is. Rainbow Way was inspired by my love of adding tons of leftovers/mini skeins. You can use all different colours, or choose just one contrast colour. Rainbow Way is a great stash buster and advent project.

YOU WILL NEED

NEEDLES

Size 2.25mm (US 1), or size needed to obtain tension, for your preferred method of knitting in the round.

NOTIONS

• Darning Needle

YARN

The sample was knitted using Lolodidit Loriginal (85% Extra Fine Superwash Merino, 15% Nylon) fingering weight, 100g (402m/440yds)

Naked Hippo (1 skein)

Lolodidit Loriginal (85% Extra Fine Superwash Merino, 15% Nylon) fingering weight, 28g (113m/124yds) in the following shades:

C1 Outrageous (red) (1 skein)

C2 Sweetness (orange) (1 skein)

C3 Oow I Feel Good (yellow) (1 skein)

C4 Elayne (green) (1 skein)

C5 Moiraine (blue) (1 skein)

C6 Big Girls Don't Cry (pink) (1 skein)

C7 Violet Beauregarde (purple) (1 skein)

SIZES

Adult Small (Adult Medium) (Adult Large)

To fit a foot circumference of approximately 7 (8) (8½)in / 18 (20.5) (21.5)cm

TENSION (GAUGE)

unblocked

36 stitches and 40 rows measure 4 x 4in (10 x 10cm) over stocking (stockinette) stitch using 2.25mm needles

PATTERN

CUFF

Using the long tail cast on (or preferred method) CO 56 (64) (72) sts. Join for working in the round taking care not to twist your stitches.

Magic Loop: Divide the stitches evenly between your two needles 28 (32) (36) sts on each needle.

DPNS: Divide the stitches evenly between your four needles 14 (16) (18) sts on each needle.

Rounds 1-12: *K2, p2; repeat from *.

Round 13: Knit all stitches.

LEG

Continue knitting with the chart until you've reached the desired length from your cast-on edge. The sample was knitted to 5½in (14cm) from the ribbing for the size Adult Small, ending on Round 10.

HEEL

The short row heel is worked on half of your stitches with your MC.

Knit across the first 28 (32) (34) sts separating the stitches into three equal parts using stitch markers. If your stitch count isn't divisible by 3, then the middle section gets more stitches. (Eg; If it's 28, then divide it as 9 / 10 / 9). Turn work.

Row 1 (WS): Ds, purl to the end, turn work.

Row 2: Ds, knit to the last ds but do not work it, turn work.

Row 3: Ds, purl to the last ds but do not work it, turn work.

Repeat Rows 2 and 3 until you have worked all the stitches on each side of the stitch markers.

You have now completed the first half of the short row heel. In this section as you come to a ds you will knit or purl it together treating it as a single stitch. (Note; Depending on your stitch count if you finish on a knit round start on Row 2 instead of Row 1).

Row 1 (RS): Knit to the first ds, knit the ds together as one st, turn work.

Row 2: Ds, purl to the first ds, purl the ds together as one st, turn work.

Row 3: Ds, knit to the first ds, knit it together as one st, repeat with the next ds, turn work.

Row 4: Ds, purl to the first ds, purl it together as one st, repeat with the next ds, turn work.

Repeat Rows 3 and 4 until you have worked all the stitches.

You are now ready to work in the round again. As your last row will be a WS row, knit one more round knitting all the ds together as you come to them.

I recommend on the following two rounds to pick up an extra stitch or two in between the heel gaps. This will help close any holes that were created. Pick up the stitches between the gap and knit them together with the first stitch on your needle.

FOOT

You will continue working the colourwork chart starting at Round 1 until you've reached 1½ (1¾) (2)in / 4 (4.5) (5)cm shorter than your foot length ending on Round 10.

TOE

Round 1: K1, ssk knit to the last 3 sts, k2tog, k1 (Repeat on both needles).

Round 2: Knit all stitches.

Magic Loop: Continue these two rounds until there are 12 (12) (16) sts left on each needle.

DPNS: Continue these two rounds until there are 6 (6) (8) sts left on each needle.

Graft together using the Kitchener stitch and weave in all ends. Block as desired.

CHART

Each square represents a stitch. Read all rows from right to left. Carry the unused strands of yarn across the WS of the work, twisting yarn after every three or four stitches to avoid long loops of yarn on the WS.

PRO TIP: *If you're new to colourwork, try on the sock as you go to see how your tension is doing. If it's too tight you may need to go up a needle size. Start the colourwork chart and repeat the 7 (8) (8) stitches around the sock changing the colour of mini skein each time. You will be working the colourwork on both the front and the back of the leg.*

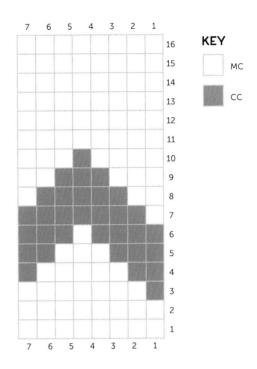

KEY

☐	MC
■	CC

PUMPKIN SPICE LATTE

Cozy up with a warm cup of pumpkin spice latte and a pair of our Pumpkin Spice Latte Socks. Inspired by my love of everything autumn (fall), these neat socks feature twisted stitches and cables. Get ready to sip on your latte while working on this fun pair of socks. Designed cuff down featuring a heel flap and gusset.

YOU WILL NEED

NEEDLES
Size 2.25mm (US 1), or size needed to obtain tension, for your preferred method of knitting in the round.

OTHER TOOLS AND MATERIALS
• Darning needle

YARN
The sample was knitted using Lizzie Anne Yarns Soft Sock (75% Wool, 25% Nylon) fingering weight, 100g (425m/465yds) 20g (85m/93yds) in Pumpkin Spice Latte Sock Set

MC: 100g skein

CC: 20g mini skein

SIZES
Adult Small (Adult Medium) (Adult Large)

To fit a foot circumference of approximately 7 (8) (8½)in / 18 (20.5) (21.5) cm

TENSION (GAUGE)
unblocked

32 stitches and 48 rows measure 4 x 4in (10 x 10cm) over stocking (stockinette) stitch using 2.25mm needles

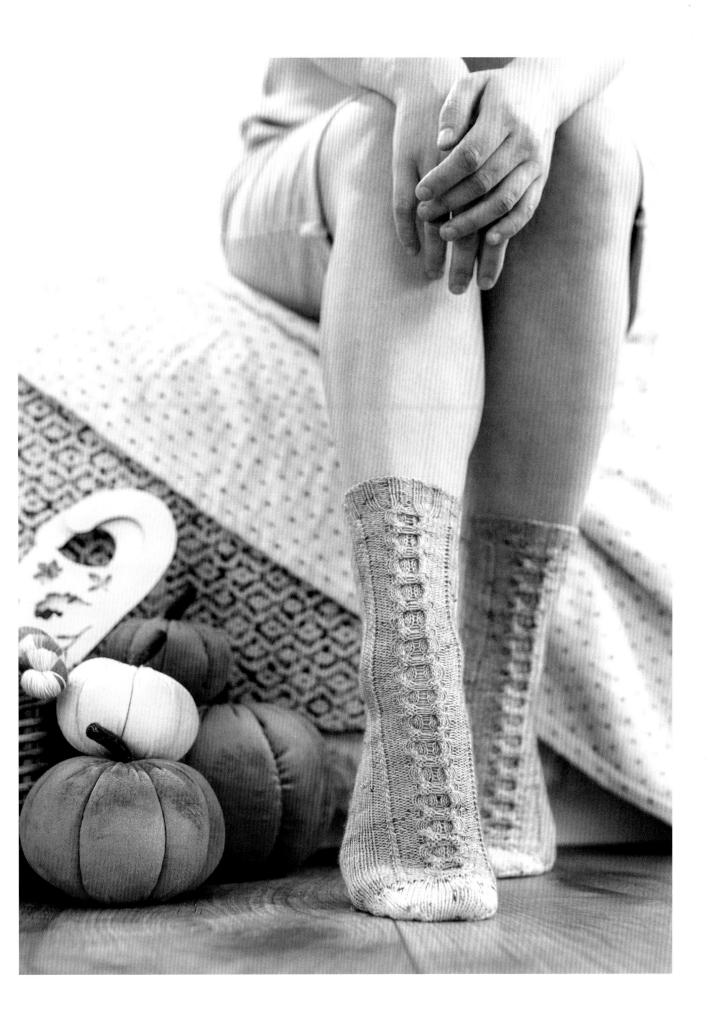

PATTERN

CUFF

Using the long tail cast on (or preferred method) CO 56 (64) (72) sts with your CC. Join for working in the round taking care not to twist your stitches.

Magic Loop: Divide the stitches evenly between your two needles 28 (32) (36) sts on each needle.

DPNS: Divide the stitches evenly between your four needles 14 (16) (18) sts on each needle.

Rounds 1-10: *K2, p2; repeat from *.

Cut CC. Leg is knit in MC.

LEG

The stitches will be divided between Needle 1 and Needle 2. Needle 1 will be the front of your foot while Needle 2 will be the back.

Use either the written or charted instructions for Needle 1.

For Needle 2: Knit all stitches.

Continue working in pattern until leg has reached the desired length ending with Round 5. The sample was knitted to 6½in (16.5cm) from the cast on.

HEEL

Heel is worked flat with your CC on Needle 1, or half the stitches: 28 (32) (36).

Row 1 (RS): *Sl1, k1; repeat from, * turn.

Row 2 (WS): Sl1, purl to end, turn.

Work Rows 1-2 a total of 15 (16) (16) times for a total of 30 (32) (32) rows.

HEEL TURN

Row 1 (RS): Sl1, k16 (18) (20), ssk, k1, turn.

Row 2 (WS): Sl1, p7, p2tog, p1, turn.

Row 3: Sl1, knit to one st before gap, ssk, k1, turn.

Row 4: Sl1, purl to one st before gap, p2tog, p1, turn.

Repeat Rows 3 and 4 until all stitches have been worked. Cut your CC.

Knit across remaining heel stitches, pick up and knit 15 (16) (16) sts along the edge of heel flap. Pick up an extra stitch on the ladder between the stitches on the row below to close any gaps. Knit across instep stitches. Pick up 16 (17) (17) sts on the other gusset side starting with the extra stitch on the ladder between the stitches on the row below to close any gaps.

GUSSET

When decreasing gusset stitches, only work decreases in Section 1 or back of heel. This is the section used to pick up all the gusset stitches. During these rounds make sure to knit all stitches on Section 2 (top of foot) without decreasing across the top of foot.

Round 1:

Section 1: K1, ssk, knit to 3 sts before the end of row, k2tog, k1.

Section 2: Knit all stitches.

Round 2:

Section 1 and 2: Knit all stitches.

Continue Rounds 1 and 2 until you've reached your original stitch count of 56 (64) (72) sts.

Continue knitting in pattern for the front of the sock until it measures 2 (2, 2½)in / 5 (5) (6.5)cm.

TOE

Toe is worked with your CC.

Round 1: K1, ssk, knit to the last 3 sts, k2tog, k1 (Repeat on both needles).

Round 2: Knit.

Magic Loop: Continue these two rounds until there are 8 (12) (12) sts left on each needle.

DPNS: Continue these two rounds until there are 4 (6) (6) sts left on each needle.

Graft together using the Kitchener stitch and weave in all ends. Block as desired.

Enjoy the process — knitting socks can be both relaxing and fun.

CHARTS

Each square represents a stitch. Read all rows from right to left.

SMALL

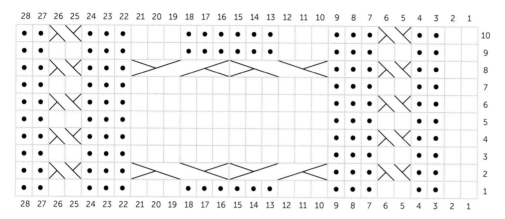

MEDIUM

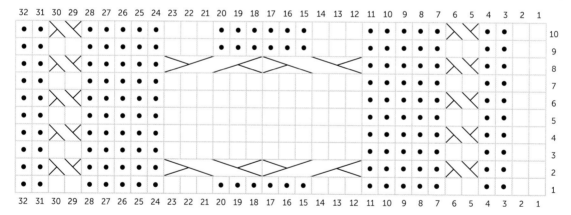

WRITTEN INSTRUCTIONS

SMALL

Round 1: K2, p2, k2, p3, k3, p6, k3, p3, k2, p2.

Round 2: K2, p2, 1/1 LC, p3, 3/3 RC, 3/3 LC, p3, 1/1 LC, p2.

Round 3: K2, p2, k2, p3, k12, p3, k2, p2.

Round 4: K2, p2, 1/1 LC, p3, k12, p3, 1/1 LC, p2.

Round 5: Repeat Round 3.

Rounds 6 and 7: Repeat Rounds 4 and 5.

Round 8: K2, p2, 1/1 LC, p3, 3/3 LC, 3/3 RC, p3, 1/1 LC, p2.

Round 9: Repeat Round 1.

Round 10: K2, p2, 1/1 LC, p3, k3, p6, k3, p3, 1/1 LC, p2.

MEDIUM

Round 1: K2, p2, k2, p5, k3, p6, k3, p5, k2, p2.

Round 2: K2, p2, 1/1 LC, p5, 3/3 RC, 3/3 LC, p5, 1/1 LC, p2.

Round 3: K2, p2, k2, p5, k12, p5, k2, p2.

Round 4: K2, p2, 1/1 LC, p5, k12, p5, 1/1 LC, p2.

Round 5: Repeat Round 3.

Rounds 6 and 7: Repeat Rounds 4 and 5.

Round 8: K2, p2, 1/1 LC, p5, 3/3 LC, 3/3 RC, p5, 1/1 LC, p2.

Round 9: Repeat Round 1.

Round 10: K2, p2, 1/1 LC, p5, k3, p6, k3, p5, 1/1 LC, p2.

LARGE

Round 1: K2, p2, k4, p5, k3, p6, k3, p5, k4, p2.

Round 2: K2, p2, 2/2 LC, p5, 3/3 RC, 3/3 LC, p5, 2/2 LC, p2.

Round 3: K2, p2, k4, p5, k12, p5, k4, p2.

Round 4: K2, p2, 2/2 LC, p5, k12, p5, 2/2 LC, p2.

Round 5: Repeat Round 3.

Rounds 6 and 7: Repeat Rounds 4 and 5.

Round 8: K2, p2, 2/2 LC, p5, 3/3 LC, 3/3 RC, p5, 2/2 LC, p2.

Round 9: Repeat Round 1.

Round 10: K2, p2, 2/2 LC, p5, k3, p6, k3, p5, 2/2 LC, p2.

LARGE

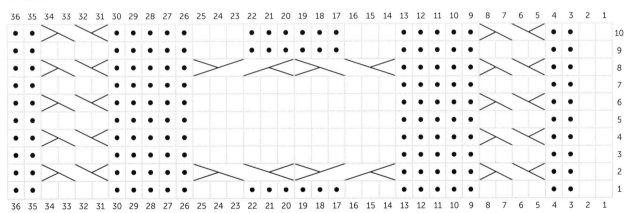

KEY

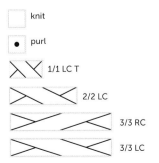

knit

● purl

1/1 LC T

2/2 LC

3/3 RC

3/3 LC

TECHNIQUES

I wanted to include some key instructions that you will need to knit socks. You can either browse through these illustrations or look them up on YouTube.

LONG TAIL CAST ON

This cast on is my favourite to use for socks since it's neat and stretchy. The quickest method to measure the length of the tail is to measure out 3.5 times the length of the final cast-on edge. As an example, if your sock circumference is 7in (18cm) you should measure out 24½ (63cm) of yarn for the tail.

1. Start by making a slip knot on your needle.

2. With your free hand you'll be inserting the thumb and finger between the strands opening your thumb and finger to create the two loops. (A)

3. Hold the needle in your right hand, swing the needle up and into the thumb loop from below (B), over and down through the finger loop. (C)

4. You will bring it back down through the thumb loop and slip the loop off the thumb, then tighten your stitches. (D)

Repeat Steps 3-4 until you've cast on the number of stitches in your pattern. Remember the slip knot counts as 1 stitch.

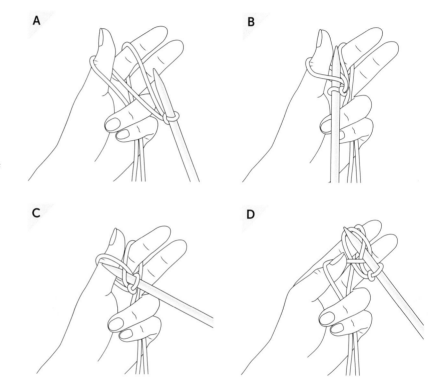

TURKISH CAST ON (TOE UP SOCKS)

We use the Turkish cast on for toe up socks. You will need a circular needle for this cast-on method.

1. Start by making a slip knot on your needle.

2. Arrange both needle tips together one on top of the other. (They will be parallel to each other, with the slipknot on the needle below, your working yarn will be towards the top and the tail will be towards the bottom.) (A)

3. Wrap the working yarn around both needles as many as half the total amount of stitches you need for casting on. (As an example, if you want to cast on 20 stitches, wrap the yarn a total of 10 times, the slip knot does not count as a stitch.) (B, C)

4. Pull out the bottom needle while holding the working yarn with your hand. (You'll be pulling out the needle with the slip knot and pulling the slip knot off.)

5. You will be using the pulled out needle to knit into the wrapped stitches. Inserting your right hand needle into the wrapped stitches knit wise, and knit this stitch. (D)

6. You will continue Step 5 until you've worked all the stitches on the left hand needle. (E)

7. Turn your work and start working on the bottom needle. You will now repeat Step 5 on the bottom needle. (F)

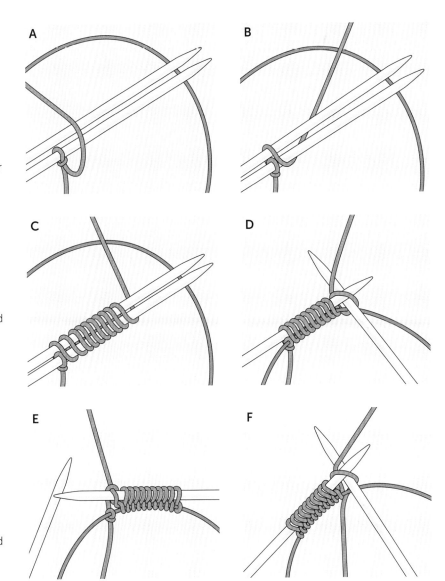

KITCHENER STITCH

The Kitchener stitch is a great way to secure and bind off the toe of your sock. You will be cutting your working yarn leaving about a 12in (30.5cm) tail and using a darning needle to graft the stitches together.

1. Put your darning needle through the first stitch on the front needle knit wise (A) and thread your yarn through leaving the stitch on the needle.

2. Then put your darning needle through the first stitch on the back needle purl wise (B) and thread your yarn through leaving the stitch on the needle.

3. Now put the darning needle back into the first stitch of the front needle but purl wise this time (C) and thread your yarn through.

4. Slip the first stitch off the front needle, then put your darning needle into the second stitch on the front needle knit wise (D) and pull the yarn through. Put your darning needle back into the first stitch on the back needle purl wise (E) and slip this one off the needle.

Repeat Steps 1-4 along the row. (F) To finish, bring the tail inside of your sock and weave in the ends.

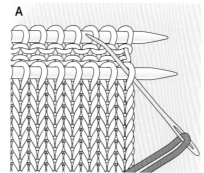

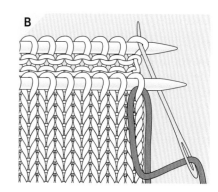

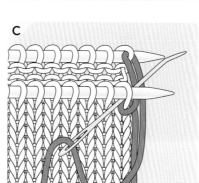

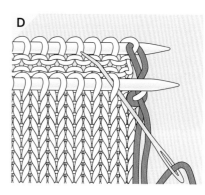

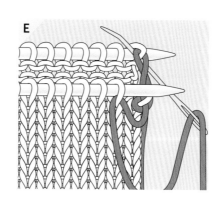

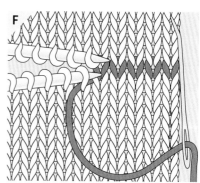

EMBROIDERY STITCH

Once the Birthday Sprinkles socks are completed you will be adding the sprinkles. These are done using scraps of yarn of the same weight. They will be embroidery stitched onto your sock.

You will be using a darning needle and some scrap yarn for the colour of the sprinkle.

1. Start by fastening your yarn at the back of the work. Poke your needle through the right side of the fabric bringing the yarn through. (A)

2. Insert the needle through a stitch diagonally from it, pulling the yarn through. (B)

3. Going back into the original stitch, bring the yarn through. (C, D)

Repeat steps 2 and 3 on the same sprinkle. Each sprinkle on the sample was embroidered twice in the same stitch.

Make sure to keep the yarn tension even.

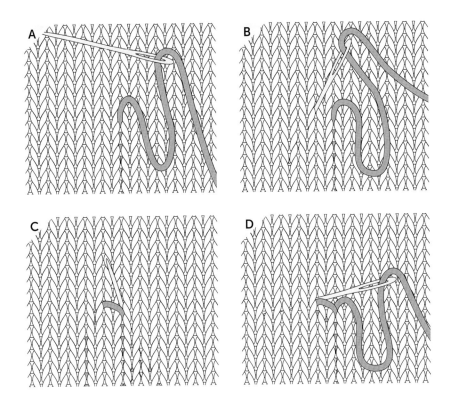

JENY'S SURPRISINGLY STRETCHY CAST (BIND) OFF FOR 1X1 RIBBING

This bind off is great for toe up socks.

1. Knit the first stitch with your yarn at the back.

2. Bring the yarn around the needle forward (creating a yarn over before your purl). (A) Purl the next stitch.

3. Take the yarn over and pass it over the purl stitch you just worked. (B) Then pass the knit stitch on the right hand needle over the purl stitch.

4. Your yarn will now be in front of your work after the purl; take it back between the needles and then over to the front (creating a backwards yarn over). (C) Knit the next stitch.

5. Pass the yarn over and the purl stitch over the knit stitch you just worked.

Repeat steps 2–5 until there is one stitch remaining, then fasten off as normal.

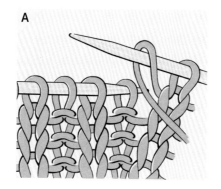

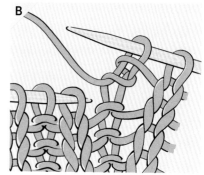

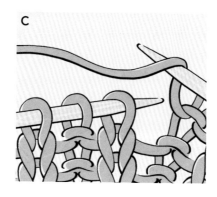

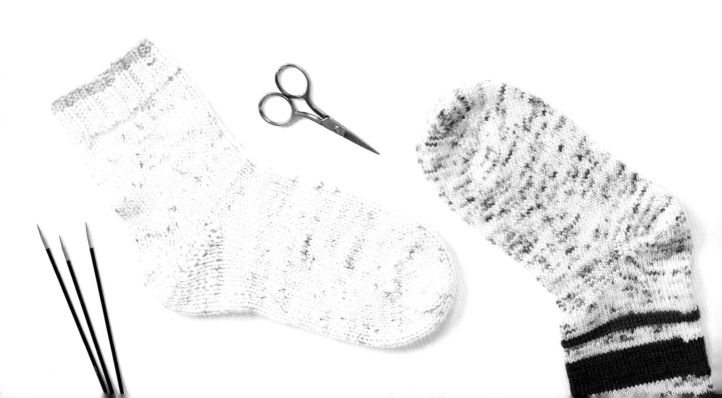

JOGLESS STRIPES

When you knit stripes you may not want to have a round that is a little higher than the other causing the pattern to have a 'jog' in the stripes. Use this following method to help create jogless stripes:

1. Knit 1 full round in your new colour.

2. Before you start the next round, use the right hand needle to pick up the right hand leg of the stitch that is just below the first stitch on the left hand needle. Place this on the left hand needle.

3. Knit these two stitches together.

HOLDING TWO YARNS TOGETHER

Some of the patterns in this book include knitting socks double stranded. This means you'll be holding 2 strands of fingering weight yarn together. 2 strands of 4ply fingering weight equal about a DK 8ply yarn.

1. Hold both strands together in your hand as you would with one strand. Go into knit your first stitch while wrapping both strands around the right hand needle at the same time.

2. When you are working the stitches, remember to work each set of double loop as 1 stitch.

WEAVING IN ENDS

When you are done with your projects it's important to have a clean look to weave in all your ends.

1. With the wrong side facing you, use a tapestry needle and thread the tail end of your yarn through the back of the purl bumps. For the best look, go the opposite direction of where you knit. This will help close any gaps in your knitting. You will need to thread about 6-10 stitches to secure the yarn. Once completed, trim the yarn close to the work.

ABOUT THE AUTHOR

My knitting journey started the same as a lot of other knitters. I saw my Nanny (Grandmother) knit slippers daily for the whole family. Every time you went to her apartment, there was a little basket at the door filled with knitted slippers. When I was 7-8, she gave me a pair of long, straight knitting needles with maybe 10-12 stitches to start a simple scarf. It wasn't long until the edges began to shift from one side to the other; suddenly, there were more stitches than fewer. After that attempt at making a scarf, I didn't try to knit again. Fast forward to 2012, I decided to teach myself to knit by watching YouTube videos. By this time, my Nanny could no longer use her hands. I was so excited to go and show her that I taught myself to knit and was able to create socks. I would love to bring her the socks and sweater I made; she was amazed by all the yarns and tools I would bring. My love of knitting came from repeatedly watching her knit the same pair of slippers.

Since then, my passion for knitting has grown, and I've created a full-time job from something I never thought imaginable. I love sharing my knitting and passion with others through my YouTube channel, Patreon group and more. I now live with my husband and twin daughters, who are all incredibly knit-worthy; I hope to one day inspire them to pick up the knitting needles as well.

I hope this book will inspire you as well.

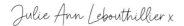

Julie Ann Lebouthillier x

ACKNOWLEDGEMENTS

Words can't describe how incredible this opportunity was for me to write my first-ever book. **I'm still pinching myself that this is happening!** I could not have done this without the incredible team at David & Charles. They made the whole journey so easy for me and made it look incredible. Thank you to Sarah, Jessica, Sam and all the fantastic team!

A massive thank you to the dyers who sent me the yarn support for this book. First, thank you to Lauriane of Tot-Le-Matin Yarns for sending me a stunning yarn bundle to help with all the new designs. I appreciate your support of me throughout the years. Thank you to Campfiber Yarns, Craftnut Yarns, Lolodid It, MoonGlow Yarn Co., and Nicole C. Méndez. I want to thank my friend Heather, who helped me knit the samples for this book; I honestly could not have done this without her.

I also want to thank my incredible husband, Eric, who has always supported me and my dreams. He's had to put up with me bringing yarn and socks everywhere and having them all over our house! Also, not to forget all the late-night freakouts, ensuring everything was going okay and on track. Thank you for being there for both me and our girls. I appreciate you more than you'll ever know. And thank you to my wonderful girls Claire and Chloe. I hope Momma showing you this book will make you reach for the stars and know you can do anything you want. Momma loves you both! And last but not least, thank you to all my incredible supporters and Patreon members. Your support means the world. THANK YOU!

INDEX

A DAVID AND CHARLES BOOK
© David and Charles, Ltd 2024

David and Charles is an imprint of David and Charles, Ltd
Suite A, Tourism House, Pynes Hill, Exeter, EX2 5WS

Text and Designs © Julie Ann Lebouthillier 2024
Layout and Photography © David and Charles, Ltd 2024

First published in the UK and USA in 2024

ISBN-13: 9781446312803 paperback
ISBN-13: 9781446312933 EPUB
ISBN-13: 9781446312940 PDF

This book has been printed on paper from approved suppliers and made from pulp from sustainable sources.

Printed in the UK by Buxton for:
David and Charles, Ltd
Suite A, Tourism House, Pynes Hill, Exeter, EX2 5WS

10 9 8 7 6 5 4 3 2

Publishing Director: Ame Verso
Senior Commissioning Editor: Sarah Callard
Managing Editor: Jeni Chown
Editor: Jessica Cropper
Project Editor: Sam Winkler
Technical Editor: Jo Carobene
Head of Design: Anna Wade
Designers: Sam Staddon & Blanche Williams
Pre-press Designer: Susan Reansbury
Illustrations: Kuo Kang Chen & Cathy Brear
Art Direction: Sarah Rowntree
Photography: Jason Jenkins
Production Manager: Beverley Richardson

David and Charles publishes high-quality books on a wide range of subjects. For more information visit www.davidandcharles.com.

Share your makes with us on social media using #dandcbooks and follow us on Facebook and Instagram by searching for @dandcbooks.

Layout of the digital edition of this book may vary depending on reader hardware and display settings.